A. C. (Augustus Charles) Thompson

Songs in the Night

Or, Hymns for the Sick and Suffering

A. C. (Augustus Charles) Thompson

Songs in the Night
Or, Hymns for the Sick and Suffering

ISBN/EAN: 9783744779357

Printed in Europe, USA, Canada, Australia, Japan

Cover: Foto ©Thomas Meinert / pixelio.de

More available books at **www.hansebooks.com**

SONGS IN THE NIGHT.

PRAYER FOR THE SICK.

"Is any sick among you? let him call for the elders of the church; and let them pray over him." — *James* v. 14.

> O Lord, our strength and righteousness,
> Our hope and refuge in distress,
>   Our Saviour and our God!
> See here, a helpless sinner see;
> Weak and in pain he looks to thee,
>   For healing in thy blood.

HYMNS.

In sickness make thou all his bed,
Thy hand support his fainting head,
   His feeble soul defend;
Teach him on thee to cast his care,
And all his grief and burden bear,
   And love him to the end.

If now thou wilt his soul require,
O, sit as a refiner's fire,
   And purge it first from sin!
Thy love hath quicker wings than Death,
The fulness of thy Spirit breathe,
   And bring thy nature in.

If in the vale of tears thy will
Appoints him to continue still,
   O, sanctify his pain!
And let him patiently submit
To suffer as thy love sees fit,
   And never once complain.

O, let him look to thee alone,
That all thy will on him be done!
   His only pleasure be,
Alike resigned to live or die,
As most thy name may glorify,
   To live or die to thee.
WESLEY.

THE REFINER'S FIRE.

"He shall sit as a refiner and purifier of silver." — *Mal.* iii. 3.

HE that from dross would win the ore
   Bends o'er the crucible an earnest eye,
The subtile, searching process to explore,
   Lest the one brilliant moment should pass by,
When in the molten, silvery, virgin mass,
He meets his pictured face as in a glass.

Thus in God's furnace are his people tried;
    Thrice happy they who to the end endure;
But who the fiery trial may abide?
    Who from the crucible come forth so pure,
That He, whose eyes of flame look through the whole,
May see his image perfect in the soul?

Nor with an evanescent glimpse alone,
    As in that mirror the refiner's face;
But, stamped with Heaven's broad signet, there be shown
    Immanuel's features full of truth and grace;
And round that seal of love this motto be,
" Not for a moment, but — Eternity!"

MONTGOMERY.

HYMNS.

GOD KNOWETH WHAT IS BEST.

"For who knoweth what is good for man in this life?" — *Eccl.* vi. 12.

WHAT, many times I musing asked, is man,
    If grief and care
Keep far from him? he knows not what he can,
    What cannot, bear.

He, till the fire hath purged him, doth remain
    Mixed all with dross:
To lack the loving discipline of pain,
    Were endless loss.

Yet when my Lord did ask me on what side
    I were content
The grief, whereby I must be purified,
    To me were sent,

HYMNS.

As each imagined anguish did appear,
    Each withering bliss
Before my soul, I cried, "O, spare me here!
    O, no, not this!"

Like one that having need of, deep within,
    The surgeon's knife,
Would hardly bear that it should graze the skin,
    Though for his life.

Nay, then, but He, who best doth understand,
    Both what we need
And what can bear, did take my case in hand,
    Nor crying heed.

HYMNS.

LOOKING UNTO JESUS.

Looking unto Jesus, the author and finisher of our faith." — *Heb.* xii. 2.

O MY soul! what means this sadness?
   Wherefore art thou thus cast down?
Let thy grief be turned to gladness;
   Bid thy restless fear be gone;
      Look to Jesus,
And rejoice in his dear name.

Though ten thousand ills beset thee,
   Though thy heart is stained with sin,
Jesus lives, he 'll ne'er forget thee,
   He will make thee pure within;
      He is faithful
To perform his gracious word.

Though distresses now attend thee,
  And thou tread'st the thorny road,
His right hand shall still defend thee;
  Soon he 'll bring thee home to God:
    Thou shalt praise him, —
  Praise the great Redeemer's name.

O that I could now adore him,
  Like the heavenly host above,
Who for ever bow before him,
  And unceasing sing his love!
    Happy spirits!
  When shall I your chorus join?

FAWCETT.

JUST AS I AM.

"Jesus, thou son of David, have mercy on me." — *Mark* x. 48.

Just as I am, — without one plea,
But that thy blood was shed for me,
And that thou bid'st me come to thee,
   O Lamb of God, I come!

Just as I am, — and waiting not
To rid my soul of one dark blot,
To thee, whose blood can cleanse each spot,
   O Lamb of God, I come!

Just as I am, — though tossed about
With many a conflict, many a doubt,
"Fightings within, and fears without,"
   O Lamb of God, I come!

Just as I am, — poor, wretched, blind;
Sight, riches, healing of the mind,
Yea, all I need in thee to find,
  O Lamb of God, I come!

Just as I am, — thou wilt receive;
Wilt welcome, pardon, cleanse, relieve;
Because thy promise I believe,
  O Lamb of God, I come!

Just as I am, — thy love unknown
Has broken every barrier down;
Now, to be thine, yea, thine alone,
  O Lamb of God, I come!
Charlotte Elliott.

SUBMISSION.

"The Lord gave, and the Lord hath taken away; blessed be the name of the Lord." — *Job* i. 21.

Submissive to thy will, my God,
    I all to thee resign,
And bow before thy chastening rod;
    I mourn, but not repine.

Why should my foolish heart complain,
    When wisdom, truth, and love
Direct the stroke, inflict the pain,
    And point to joys above.

How short are all my sufferings here,
    How needful every cross;
Away, my unbelieving fear,
    Nor call my gain my loss.

Then give, O Lord, or take away,
  I 'll bless thy sacred name;
Jesus, to-day, and yesterday,
  And ever, is the same.

HAWEIS.

HE WHOM CHRIST LOVES.

"Lord, behold, he whom thou lovest is sick"—*John* xi. 8.

SAVIOUR! I can welcome sickness,
  If these words be said of me;
Can rejoice, 'midst pain and weakness,
  If I am but loved by thee;
    Love so precious
Balm for every wound will be.

Thou, who waitest not for fitness
  In the souls thy blood has saved,
Let thy Spirit now bear witness,
  He this sentence has engraved,—

Love so precious
Gives me all my prayers have craved.

Though that love send days of sadness,
   In a life so brief as this,
It prepares me days of gladness,
   And a life of perfect bliss;
     Love so precious
Bids me every fear dismiss.

"GOD IS LOVE."

1 *John* iv. 8.

I CANNOT always trace the way
   Where thou, Almighty One, dost move;
But I can always, always say,
     That God is love.

When fear her chilling mantle flings
    O'er earth, my soul to heaven above,
As to her sanctuary, springs,
    For God is love,

When mystery clouds my darkened path,
    I'll check my dread, my doubts reprove;
In this my soul sweet comfort hath,
    That God is love.

The entanglement which restless thought,
    Mistrust, and idle reasoning wove,
Are thus unravelled and unwrought, —
    For God is love.

Yes, God is love, — a thought like this
    Can every gloomy thought remove,
And turn all tears, all woes, to bliss,
    For God is love.

BOWRING.

PILGRIM! IS THY JOURNEY DREAR?

"Leave me not, neither forsake me, O God of my salvation!" — *Ps.* xxvii. 9.

Pilgrim! is thy journey drear?
   Are its lights extinct for ever?
Still suppress the rising fear, —
   God forsakes the righteous, never!

Storms may gather o'er thy path,
   All the ties of life may sever;
Still, amid the fear and death,
   God forsakes the righteous, never!

Pain may rack thy wasting frame,
   Health desert thy couch for ever,
Faith still burns with deathless flame,
   God forsakes the righteous, never!

Mrs. Southey.

STRENGTH ACCORDING TO THE DAY.

" As thy days, so shall thy strength be."— Deut. xxxiii. 25.

Wait, my soul, upon the Lord,
  To his gracious promise flee,
Laying hold upon his word,
  " As thy day, thy strength shall be."

If the sorrows of thy case
  Seem peculiar still to thee,
God has promised needful grace, —
  " As thy day, thy strength shall be."

Days of trial, days of grief,
  In succession thou mayst see;
This is still thy sweet relief, —
  " As thy day, thy strength shall be."

HYMNS.

Rock of Ages, I 'm secure,
  With thy promise full and free;
Faithful, positive, and sure,
  " As thy day, thy strength shall be."

TRIALS A BLESSING.

"Count it all joy when ye fall into divers temptations." — *James* 1. 2.

'T is my happiness below,
  Not to live without the cross,
But the Saviour's power to know,
  Sanctifying every loss.
Trials must and will befall,
  But with humble faith to see
Love inscribed upon them all,
  This is happiness to me.

God in Israel sows the seeds
   Of affliction, pain, and toil;
These spring up and choke the weeds,
   Which would else o'erspread the soil.
Trials make the promise sweet,
   Trials give new life to prayer,
Trials bring me to his feet,
   Lay me low, and keep me there.

Did I meet no trials here,
   No correction by the way,
Might I not, with reason, fear
   I should prove a castaway?
Worldlings may escape the rod,
   Sunk in earthly, vain delight;
But the true-born child of God
   Must not, would not, if he might.

COWPER.

THANKFUL AND UNTHANKFUL.

"For as he thinketh in his heart, so is he." — Prov. xxiii 7.

Some murmur when their sky is clear,
    And wholly bright to view,
If one small speck of dark appear
    In their great heaven of blue;
And some with thankful love are filled,
    If but one streak of light,
One ray of God's good mercy, gild
    The darkness of their night.

In palaces are hearts that ask,
    In discontent and pride,
Why life is such a dreary task,
    And all good things denied:
And hearts in poorest huts admire
    How love has in their aid
(Love, that not ever seems to tire)
    Such rich provision made.

R. C. Trench.

THE FOUNTAIN.

"In that day there shall be a fountain opened to the house of David, and to the inhabitants of Jerusalem, for sin and for uncleanness." — *Zech.* xiii. 1.

Come to Calvary's holy mountain,
    Sinners! ruined by the fall;
Here a pure and healing fountain
    Flows to you, to me, to all, —
In a full, perpetual tide,
Opened when the Saviour died.

Come, in poverty and meanness,
    Come, defiled without, within;
From infection and uncleanness,
    From the leprosy of sin,
Wash your robes and make them white;
Ye shall walk with God in light.

Come, in sorrow and contrition,
    Wounded, impotent, and blind;
Here the guilty, free remission,
    Here the troubled, peace may find:
Health this fountain will restore;
He that drinks will thirst no more.

He that drinks shall live for ever;
    'T is a soul-renewing flood;
God is faithful, — God will never
    Break his covenant in blood,
Signed when our Redeemer died,
Sealed when he was glorified!

                              MONTGOMERY.

COME UNTO ME.

"Come unto me, all ye that labor and are heavy laden, and I will give you rest." — *Matt.* xi. 28.

With tearful eyes I look around,
  Life seems a dark and stormy sea;
Yet 'midst the gloom I hear a sound,
  A heavenly whisper, "Come to me!"

It tells me of a place of rest, —
  It tells me where my soul may flee;
O, to the weary, faint, oppressed,
  How sweet the bidding, "Come to me."

When nature shudders, loth to part,
  From all I love, enjoy, and see;
When a faint chill steals o'er my heart,
  A sweet voice utters, "Come to me!"

"Come, for all else must fail and die;
  Earth is no resting-place for thee;
Heavenward direct thy weeping eye,
  I am thy portion, "Come to me!"

O voice of mercy! voice of love!
  In conflict, grief, and agony;
Support me, cheer me from above!
  And gently whisper, "Come to me!"

THE SAVIOUR'S INVITATION.

"Come unto me, all ye that labor and are heavy laden, and I will give you rest" — *Matt.* xi. 28.

How sweetly flowed the Gospel's sound
  From lips of gentleness and grace,
When listening thousands gathered round,
  And joy and reverence filled the place!

From heaven he came, of heaven he spoke,
    To heaven he leads his followers' way;
Dark clouds of gloomy night he broke,
    Unveiling an immortal day.

"Come, wanderers, to my Father's home,
    Come, all ye weary ones, and rest";
Yes! sacred Teacher, we will come,—
    Obey thee, love thee, and be blest!

Decay, then, tenements of dust,
    Pillars of earthly pride, decay!
A nobler mansion waits the just,
    And Jesus has prepared the way.

BOWRING.

SUFFICIENT GRACE.

"O bring me out of my distresses!" — *Ps.* xxv. 17.

AND wilt thou hear the fevered heart
    To thee in silence cry?
And as th' inconstant wildfires dart
    Out of the restless eye,
Wilt thou forgive the wayward thought,
By kindly woes yet half untaught,
A Saviour's right so dearly bought,
    That hope should never die?

Thou, who didst sit on Jacob's well,
    The weary hour of noon,
The languid pulses thou canst tell,
    The nerveless spirit tune.
Thou, from whose cross in anguish burst
The cry that owned thy dying thirst,

To thee we turn, our last and first,
    Our Sun and soothing Moon.

From darkness here, and dreariness,
    We ask not full repose,
Only be thou at hand, to bless
    Our trial hour of woes.
Is not the pilgrim's toil o'erpaid
By the clear rill and palmy shade?
And see we not, up earth's dark glade,
    The gate of heaven unclose?

KEBLE.

HYMNS.

"THY WILL BE DONE."
Matt. vi. 10.

WHAT though in lonely grief I sigh
For friends beloved, no longer nigh;
Submissive still would I reply,
　"Thy will be done!"

If thou shouldst call me to resign
What most I prize, it ne'er was mine;
I only yield thee what was thine, —
　"Thy will be done!"

Should pining sickness waste away
My life in premature decay,
My Father! still I strive to say,
　"Thy will be done!"

HYMNS.

If but my fainting heart be blest
With thy sweet Spirit for its guest,
My God! to thee I leave the rest, —
"Thy will be done!"

Renew my will from day to day,
Blend it with thine, and take away
All that now makes it hard to say,
"Thy will be done!"

DIVINE PEACE.

"The peace of God which passeth all understanding." — *Phil.* iv. 7.

Peace of God, which knows no measure,
  Heavenly sunbeam of the soul,
Peace beyond all earthly treasure,
  Come, and every fear control.

Do disease and pain alarm me,
 Do I fear impending ill?
Evil hath not power to harm me,
 He can whisper, " Peace, be still!"

O Almighty to deliver!
 Thou on whom my hope is stayed,
I would trust in thee for ever,
 Then I cannot be afraid.

SICKNESS SANCTIFIED.

"I know, O Lord, that thy judgments are right, and that thou in faithfulness hast afflicted me." — *Ps.* cxix. 75.

For what shall I praise thee, my God and my King?
For what blessings the tribute of gratitude bring?
Shall I praise thee for pleasure, for health, and for ease?
For the spring of delight, and the sunshine of peace?

Shall I praise thee for flowers that bloomed on my breast?
For joys in perspective, and pleasures possessed?
For the spirits that heightened my day of delight,
And the slumbers that sat on my pillow by night?

For this should I praise thee! but if only for this,
I should leave half untold the donation of bliss;
I thank thee for sickness, for sorrow, for care,
For the thorns I have gathered, the anguish I bear;

For the nights of anxiety, watchings, and tears,
A present of pain, a perspective of fears;
I praise thee, I bless thee, my King and my God,
For the good and the evil thy love hath bestowed.

The flowers were sweet, but their fragrance is flown
They yielded no fruits, they are withered and gone;
The thorn it was poignant, but precious to me, —
'T was the message of mercy, it led me to thee.

C. Fry.

EXTREME SUFFERINGS.

"Save me, O God! for the waters are come in unto my soul." —*Ps.* lxix. 1.

Full of trembling expectation,
   Feeling much, and fearing more,
Mighty God of my salvation!
   I thy timely aid implore;
Suffering Son of Man, be near me,
   All my sufferings to sustain;
By thy sorer griefs to cheer me,
   By thy more than mortal pain.

Call to mind that unknown anguish
   In thy days of flesh below;
When thy troubled soul did languish
   Under a whole world of woe;
When thou didst our curse inherit,
   Groan beneath our guilty load,
Burdened with a wounded spirit,
   Bruised by all the wrath of God.

By thy most severe temptation,
  In that dark, satanic hour;
By thy last, mysterious passion,
  Screen me from the adverse power.
By thy fainting in the garden,
  By thy bloody sweat, I pray,
Write upon my heart the pardon,
  Take my sins and fears away.

By the travail of thy spirit,
  By thine outcry on the tree,
By thine agonizing merit,
  In my pangs, remember me!
By thy death I thee conjure,
  A weak, dying soul befriend;
Make me patient to endure,
  Make me faithful to the end.

C. WESLEY.

SUFFERING SANCTIFIED.

"I take pleasure in infirmities."—2 *Cor.* xii. 10.

How happy the sorrowful man,
   Whose sorrow is sent from above,
Awaked by a visit of pain,
   Chastised by omnipotent love!
The author of all his distress,
   He comes by affliction to know;
And God he in heaven shall bless,
   That ever he suffered below.

Thus, thus may I happily grieve,
   And hear the intent of his rod;
The marks of adoption receive,
   The strokes of a merciful God;
With nearer access to his throne,
   My burden of follies confess,
The cause of my miseries own,
   And cry for an answer of peace.

O Father of mercies! on me,
　On me in affliction bestow
A power of applying to thee,
　A sanctified use of my woe.
I would, in a spirit of prayer,
　To all thine appointments submit,
The pledge of my happiness bear,
　And joyfully die at thy feet.
WESLEY.

REMEMBERED AFFLICTIONS.

"Thou, which hast showed me great and sore troubles, shalt quicken me again and shalt bring me up again from the depths of the earth." — *Ps.* lxxi. 20.

I CANNOT call affliction sweet,
　And yet 't was good to bear;
Affliction brought me to thy feet,
　And I found comfort there.

My wearied soul was all resigned
    To thy most gracious will;
O had I kept that better mind,
    Or been afflicted still!

Where are the vows which then I vowed?
    The joys which then I knew?
Those, vanished like the morning cloud;
    These, like the morning dew.

Lord, grant me grace for every day,
    Whate'er my state may be,
'Through life, in death, with truth to say,
    My God is all to me.
MONTGOMERY.

REJOICING IN HOPE.

Know, my soul, thy full salvation,
   Rise o'er sin, and fear, and care;
Joy to find, in every station,
   Something still to do or bear:
Think what Spirit dwells within thee;
   Think what Father's smiles are thine;
Think what Jesus did to win thee;
   Child of heaven! canst thou repine?

Haste thee on from grace to glory,
   Armed with faith and winged with prayer;
Heaven's eternal day 's before thee,
   God's own hand shall guide thee there;
Soon shall close thine earthly mission,
   Soon shall pass thy pilgrim days;
Hope shall change to glad fruition,
   Faith to sight, and prayer to praise.

GRANT.

"MY TIMES ARE IN THY HAND."

Ps. xxxi. 15.

"My times are in thy hand,"
　My God, I'd have them there;
My life, my friends, my soul, I leave
　Entirely to thy care.

"My times are in thy hand,"
　Whatever they may be;
Pleasing or painful, dark or bright,
　As best may seem to thee.

"My times are in thy hand,"
　Why should I doubt or fear?
My Father's hand will never cause
　His child a needless tear.

"My times are in thy hand,"
I'll always trust in thee;
And after death, at thy right hand
I shall for ever be.

WHOLLY RESIGNED.

*For he maketh sore, and bindeth up; he woundeth, and his hands make whole." — *Job* v. 18.

My whole, though broken heart, O Lord,
    From henceforth shall be thine,
And here I do my vow record,
    This hand, these words, are mine.
All that I have, without reserve
    I offer here to thee,
Thy will and honor all shall serve
    That thou bestow'dst on me.

Now it belongs not to my share,
    Whether I die or live,
To love and serve thee is my share,
    And this thy grace must give.
If life be long, I will be glad,
    That I may long obey;
If short, yet why should I be sad,
    That shall have the same pay?

If death shall bruise this springing seed,
    Before it comes to fruit,
The will with thee goes for the deed,
    Thy life was in the root.
Long life is a long grief and toil,
    And multiplieth faults;
In long wars, he may have the foil,
    That 'scapes in short assaults.

Christ leads us through no darker rooms
    Than he went through before.
He that into God's kingdom comes,
    Must enter by this door.
Come, Lord, when grace hath made me meet
    Thy blessed face to see,
For if thy work on earth be sweet,
    What will thy glory be!

Then I shall end my sad complaints,
    And weary, sinful days,
And join with the triumphant saints,
    That sing Jehovah's praise.
My knowledge of that life is small,
    The eye of faith is dim,
But 't is enough that Christ knows all,
    And I shall be with him.

BAXTER.

SELF-RENUNCIATION.

"That the name of our Lord Jesus Christ may be glorified in you, and ye n him, according to the grace of our God, and the Lord Jesus Christ." — 2 *Thess.* i. 12.

When, my Saviour, shall I be
Perfectly resigned to thee?
Poor and blind in my own eyes,
Only in thy wisdom wise?

Only thee content to know,
Ignorant of all below?
Only guided by thy light,
Only mighty in thy might?

So I may thy Spirit know,
Let him as he listeth blow;
Let the manner be unknown,
So I may with thee be one.

Fully in my life express
All the heights of holiness;
Sweetly let my spirit prove
All the depths of humble love.

WESLEY.

LITANY TO THE HOLY SPIRIT.

"Likewise also the Spirit helpeth our infirmities." — *Rom.* viii. 26.

In the hour of my distress,
When temptations me oppress,
And when I my sins confess, —
   Sweet Spirit, comfort me.

When I lie within my bed,
Sick in heart, and sick in head,
And with doubts disquieted, —
   Sweet Spirit, comfort me.

When the house doth sigh and weep,
And the world is drowned in sleep,
Yet mine eyes the watch do keep, —
　　Sweet Spirit, comfort me.

When the tempter me pursueth,
With the sins of all my youth,
And condemns me with untruth, —
　　Sweet Spirit, comfort me.

When the flames and hellish cries
Fright mine ears, and fright mine eyes,
And all terrors me surprise, —
　　Sweet Spirit, comfort me.

When the judgment is revealed,
And that opened which was sealed,
When to thee I have appealed, —
　　Sweet Spirit, comfort me.

HERRICK.

'T IS I, BE NOT AFRAID.

"Jesus spake unto them, saying, Be of good cheer; it is I, be not afraid."
Matt. xiv. 27.

WHEN waves of trouble round me swell,
   My soul is not dismayed;
I hear a voice I know full well, —
   " 'T is I, be not afraid."

When black the threatening skies appear,
   And storms my path invade,
Those accents tranquillize each fear, —
   " 'T is I, be not afraid."

There is a gulf, that must be crossed;
   Saviour, be near to aid!
Whisper, when my frail bark is tossed, —
   " ' 'T is I, be not afraid."

There is a dark and fearful vale,
   Death hides within its shade;
O, say, when flesh and heart shall fail, —
   " 'T is I, be not afraid."

FIRST REQUESTS.

"Ask what I shall give thee."—1 *Kings* iii. 5.

AND dost thou say, "Ask what thou wilt?"
   Lord, I would seize the golden hour, —
I pray to be released from guilt,
   And freed from sin and Satan's power

More of thy presence, Lord, impart,
   More of thine image let me bear;
Erect thy throne within my heart,
   And reign without a rival there.

Give me to read my pardon, sealed,
   And from thy joy to draw my strength;
To have thy boundless love revealed,
   In all its height, and breadth, and length.

Grant these requests, I ask no more,
   But to thy care the rest resign;
Sick or in health, or rich or poor,
   All shall be well, if thou art mine.

NEWTON.

THE MERCY-SEAT.

"And there I will meet with thee, and I will commune with thee from above the mercy-seat." — *Exod.* xxv. 22.

From every stormy wind that blows,
From every swelling tide of woes,
There is a calm, a sure retreat, —
'T is found beneath the " Mercy-seat."

There is a place where Jesus sheds
The oil of gladness on our heads;
A place than all beside more sweet,
It is the blood-bought " Mercy-seat."

There is a place where spirits blend,
Where friend holds fellowship with friend,
Though sundered far, — by faith they meet
Around one common " Mercy-seat."

Ah! whither could we flee for aid,
When tempted, desolate, dismayed,
Or how the host of hell defeat,
Had suffering saints no " Mercy-seat " ?

There, there on eagle wings we soar,
And sin and sense molest no more,
And heaven comes down our souls to greet,
And glory crowns the " Mercy-seat."

O, let my hand forget her skill,
My tongue be silent, cold, and still,
This throbbing heart forget to beat,
If I forget the " Mercy-seat."

       Stowell.

LONGING FOR GOD.

Ps. xlii.

Lone, amidst the dead and dying
 Lord, my spirit faints for thee,
Longing, thirsting, drooping, sighing,—
 When shall I thy presence see?

O, how altered my condition!
 Late I led the joyous throng;
Beat my heart with full fruition,
 Flowed my lips with grateful song.

Now the storm goes wildly o'er me,
 Waves on waves my soul confound;
Naught but boding fears before me,
 Naught but threatening foes around.

Save me, save me, O my Father!
 To thy faithful word I cling;
Thence, my soul, thy comfort gather;
 Hope, and thou again shalt sing.
LYTE.

ENDURING TRUST.

"For this God is our God, for ever and ever; he will be our guide even unto death."— *Ps.* xlviii. 14.

O LORD, my best desire fulfil,
 And help me to resign
Life, health, and comfort to thy will,
 And make thy pleasure mine.

Why should I shrink at thy command,
   Whose love forbids my fears;
Or tremble at the gracious hand
   That wipes away my tears?

No, let me rather freely yield
   What most I prize to thee,
Who never hast a good withheld,
   Or wilt withhold, from me.

Thy favor all my journey through,
   Thou hast engaged to grant;
What else I want, or think I do,
   'T is better still to want.

Wisdom and mercy guide my way.
   Shall I resist them both?
The poor, blind creature of a day.
   And crushed before the moth!

But ah! my inward spirit cries, —
　Still bind me to thy sway;
Else the next cloud that veils my skies
　Drives all these thoughts away.

COWPER.

"THOU HAST BEEN MY REFUGE."

Ps. lxix. 16.

O STRANGE infirmity! to think
That he will leave my soul to sink
　In darkness and distress,
Who has appeared in times of old,
Who saved me while the billows rolled,
　And cheered me with his grace.

What sweeter pledge could God bestow,
Of help in future scenes of woe,
   Than grace already given?
But unbelief, that hateful thing,
Oft makes me sigh, when I should sing
   Of confidence in Heaven!

SEARLE.

RESTING ON GOD.

"My meditation of him shall be sweet; I will be glad in the Lord." — Ps. civ. 34.

WHEN languor and disease invade
   This trembling house of clay,
'T is sweet to look beyond my pain,
   And long to fly away: —

Sweet to look inward, and attend
  The whispers of his love;
Sweet to look upward, to the place
  Where Jesus pleads above: —

Sweet to look back, and see my name
  In life's fair book set down;
Sweet to look forward, and behold
  Eternal joys my own: —

Sweet to reflect how grace divine
  My sins on Jesus laid;
Sweet to remember that his blood
  My debt of suffering paid: —

Sweet in his righteousness to stand,
  Whose love can never end;
Sweet on his covenant of grace
  For all things to depend: —

HYMNS.

Sweet on his faithfulness to rest,
   Whose love can never end;
Sweet on the covenant of his grace
   For all things to depend :—

Sweet in the confidence of faith,
   To trust his firm decrees;
Sweet to lie passive in his hands,
   And know no will but his :—

'T is sweet to rest in lively hope,
   That, when my change shall come,
Angels will hover round my bed,
   And waft my spirit home.

Then shall my disembodied soul
   Behold him and adore;
Be with his likeness satisfied,
   And grieve and sin no more.
                        TOPLADY

"BE STILL, AND KNOW THAT I AM GOD"
Ps. xlvi. 10.

When I can trust my all with God,
   In trial's fearful hour, —
Bow, all resigned, beneath his rod,
   And bless his sparing power, —
A joy springs up amid distress,
A fountain in the wilderness.

O, to be brought to Jesus' feet,
   Though sorrows fix me there,
Is still a privilege, — and sweet
   The energies of prayer,
Though sighs and tears its language be,
If Christ be nigh, and smile on me!

O, blessèd be the hand that gave ;
   Still blessèd when it takes : —
Blessèd be he who smites to save,
   Who heals the heart he breaks :
Perfect and true are all his ways,
Whom heaven adores, and death obeys.

CONDER.

"LORD, AND WHAT SHALL THIS MAN DO?"

John xxi. 21.

" Lord, and what shall this man do ? "
   Ask'st thou, Christian, for thy friend ?
If his love for Christ be true,
   Christ hath told thee of his end :
This is he whom God approves,
This is he whom Jesus loves.

Ask not of him more than this,
    Leave it in his Saviour's breast, —
Whether, early called to bliss,
    He in youth shall find his rest, —
Or, armèd in his station, wait,
Till his Lord be at the gate.

Whether in his lonely course,
    (Lonely, not forlorn,) he stay,
Or, with love's supporting force,
    Cheat the toil and cheer the way:
Leave it all in his high hand,
Who doth hearts, as streams, command.

Gales from heaven, if so he will,
    Sweeter melodies can wake
On the lonely mountain rill,
    Than the meeting waters make.
Who hath the Father and the Son
May be left, — but not alone.

Sick or healthful, slave or free,
  Wealthy, or despised and poor, —
What is that to him or thee,
  So his love to Christ endure?
When the shore is won at last,
Who will count the billows past?

Only, since our souls will shrink
  At the touch of natural grief,
When our earthly, loved ones sink,
  Lend us, Lord, thy sure relief;
Patient hearts, their pain to see,
And thy grace, to follow thee.
Keble.

WHO IS ALONE?

"Surely the Lord is in this place." — *Gen.* xxviii. 16.

How heavily the path of life
  Is trod by him who walks alone;
Who hears not, on his dreary way,
  Affection's sweet and cheering tone;
Alone, — although his heart shall bound
  With love to all things great and fair, —
They love him not, — there is not one
  His sorrow or his joy to share.

The ancient stars look coldly down
  On man, the creature of a day;
They lived before him, and live on,
  Till his remembrance pass away.
The mountain lifts its hoary head,
  Nor to his homage deigns reply;
The stormy billows bear him forth, —
  Regardless which, — to live or die.

The floweret blooms unseen by him,
    Unmindful of his warmest praise;
And, if it fades, seeks not his hand,
    Its drooping loveliness to raise.
The brute creation own his power,
    And, grateful, serve him, though in fear;
Yet cannot sympathize with man;
    For, if he weeps, they shed no tear.

Alone, — though in the busy town,
    Where hundreds hurry to and fro, —
If there is none, who, for his sake,
    A selfish pleasure would forego; —
And, O, how lonely among those
    Who have not skill to read his heart,
When first he learns how summer friends,
    At sight of wintry storms, depart!

My Saviour! and didst thou, too, feel
    How sad it is to be alone;
Deserted, in the adverse hour,
    By those who most thy love had known?
The gloomy path, though distant still,
    Was ever present to thy view;
O, how couldst thou, foreseeing it,
    For us that painful course pursue?

Forsaken by thy nearest friends,
    Surrounded by malicious foes,
No kindly voice encouraged thee,
    When the loud shout of scorn uprose.
Yet there was calm within thy soul;
    Nor stoic pride that calmness kept;
Nor Godhead unapproached by woe, —
    Like man, thou hadst both loved and wept.

Thou wert not then alone, — for God
    Sustained thee by his mighty power;
His arm most felt, his care most seen,
    When needed most, in saddest hour.
None else could comfort, none else knew
    How dreadful was the curse of sin;
He who controlled the storm without,
    Could gently whisper peace within.

Who is alone, if God be nigh?
    Who shall repine at loss of friends,
While he has one of boundless power,
    Whose constant kindness never ends?
Whose presence, felt, enhances joy,
    Whose love can stop each flowing tear,
And cause, upon the darkest cloud,
    The pledge of mercy to appear?

GOD NEVER FAILETH.

"Doth his promise fail for evermore."— Ps. lxxvii. 8.

LIFE nor death shall us dissever
From His love, who reigns for ever;
Will he fail us? never, never!
    When to him we cry.

Sin may seek to snare us,
Fury, passion, tear us!
Doubt and fear, and dark despair,
    Their fangs against us try.

But his might shall still defend us,
And his blessèd Son befriend us,
And his Holy Spirit send us
    Comfort, ere we die.

LORD, I BELIEVE.

"Lord, I believe ; help thou mine unbelief." — Mark ix. 24.

Yes, I do feel, my God, that I am thine ;
  Thou art my joy, — myself, mine only grief ;
Hear my complaint, low bending at thy shrine, —
  " Lord, I believe ; help thou mine unbelief."

Unworthy even to approach so near,
  My soul lies trembling like a summ 's leaf ;
Yet, O, forgive ! I doubt not, though I fear, —
  " Lord, I believe ; help thou mine unbelief."

True, I am weak, ah ! very weak ; but then
  I know the source whence I can draw relief ;
And, though repulsed, I still can plead again, —
  " Lord, I believe ; help thou mine unbelief."

O, draw me nearer; for, too far away,
　The beamings of thy brightness are too brief;
While faith, though fainting, still have strength to pray,—
"Lord, I believe; help thou mine unbelief."
Monsell.

CHEERFUL AND SAD.

"Is any among you afflicted? let him pray. Is any merry? let him sing psalms." — *James* v. 13.

Wake now, my soul, and humbly hear
　What thy mild Lord commands;
Each word of his will charm thine ear,
　Each word will guide thy hands.

Hark how his sweet and tender care
　Complies with our weak minds;
Whate'er our state and tempers are,
　Still some fit work he finds.

They that are merry, let them sing,
    And let the sad hearts pray;
Let those still ply their cheerful wing,
    And these their sober way.

So mounts the early, chirping lark,
    Still upwards to the skies;
So sits the turtle in the dark,
    Sighing out groans and cries.

And yet the lark, and yet the dove,
    Both sing through several parts;
And so should we, howe'er we move,
    With light or heavy hearts.

Or, rather, both should both assay,
    And their cross-notes unite;
Both grief and joy should sing and pray,
    Since both such hopes invite.

Hopes, that all present sorrow heal,
    All present joy transcend;
Hopes to possess, and taste, and feel,
    Delights that never end.

All glory to the Sacred Three,
    All honor, power, and praise;
As at the first, may ever be,
    Beyond the end of days.

PRESUMPTION AND DESPAIR.

"And in my prosperity I said, I shall never be moved." — *Ps.* xxx. 6.

One time I was allowed to steer
  Through realms of azure light;
Henceforth, I said, I need not fear
  A lower, meaner flight;
But here shall evermore abide,
In light and splendor glorified.

My heart one time the rivers fed,
  Large dews upon it lay;
A freshness it has won, I said,
  Which shall not pass away;
But what it is, it shall remain,
Its freshness to the end retain.

But when I lay upon the shore,
    Like some poor, wounded thing,
I deemed I should not evermore
    Refit my shattered wing;
Nailed to the ground, and fastened there,
This was the thought of my despair.

And, when my very heart seemed dried,
    And parched as summer dust,
Such still I deemed it must abide,
    No hope had I, no trust
That any power again could bless
With fountains that waste wilderness.

But if both hope and fear were vain,
    And came alike to naught,
Two lessons we from this may gain,
    If aught *can* teach us aught, —
One lesson rather, — to divide
Between our fearfulness and pride.

                      TRENCH.

"I AM LIKE A BROKEN VESSEL."

Ps. xxxi. 12.

O Thou, whose wise, paternal love
    Hath brought my active vigor down, —
Thy choice I thankfully approve;
    And, prostrate at thy gracious throne,
I offer up my life's remains;
I *choose* the state my God ordains.

Cast as a broken vessel by,
    Thy will I can no longer do;
Yet, while a daily death I die,
    Thy power I may in weakness show;
My patience may thy glory raise, —
My speechless woe proclaim thy praise.

But since, without thy Spirit's might,
    Thou know'st I nothing can endure,
The help I ask, in Jesus' right,
    The strength he did for me procure,
Father, abundantly impart,
And arm with love my feeble heart.

O, let me live, of thee possessed,
    In weakness, weariness, and pain;
The anguish of my laboring breast,
    The daily cross I still sustain,
For him that languished on the tree, —
    But lived, before he died, for me.

STEELE.

CHRIST MY REFUGE.

"Who have fled for refuge to lay hold upon the hope set before us." — *Heb.* vi. 18.

Jesus, lover of my soul!
   Let me to thy bosom fly;
While the nearer waters roll,
   While the tempest still is high.
Hide me, O my Saviour, hide,
   Till the storm of life be past!
Safe into the haven guide;
   O, receive my soul at last!

Other refuge have I none;
   Hangs my helpless soul on thee;
Leave, ah! leave me not alone, —
   Still support and comfort me.
All my trust on thee is stayed;
   All my help from thee I bring;
Cover my defenceless head
   With the shadow of thy wing.

Thou, O Christ! art all I want:
   More than all in thee I find.
Raise the fallen, cheer the faint,
   Heal the sick, and lead the blind.
Just-and holy is thy name:
   I am all unrighteousness,
False, and full of sin I am:
   Thou art full of truth and grace.

Plenteous grace with thee is found;
   Grace, to cover all my sin.
Let the healing streams abound,—
   Make, and keep me pure within;
Thou of life the fountain art,—
   Freely let me take of thee;
Spring thou up within my heart,—
   Rise, to all eternity.

C. WESLEY.

GO AND TELL JESUS.

" And they came unto him from every quarter." — *Mark.* i. 45.

Go and tell Jesus when thy heart is glad,
And hope and joy and friendship crowd thy way.
Ask for his sanctifying grace o'er all,
That naught may cause thy heart from him to stray.
Go and tell Jesus, making joy more bright,
Shedding o'er all thy path a holy light.

Go and tell Jesus when thy sins arise
In dread and dark perspective to thy sight,
Saviour, I am unclean, unclean, O, save!
O, cheer my gloomy way with thy clear light!
Go and tell Jesus, — he will speak to thee.
Be of good cheer, — thy sins shall pardoned be.

Go and tell Jesus when thy heart is full
Of keen and bitter agony and woe; —
When the dear, precious form of one beloved
Is parted from thee, — in the grave laid low.
Go and tell Jesus, — he will soothe thy grief,
To thy poor, suffering spirit give relief.

Go and tell Jesus when thy weak heart fails,
In looking through the mist of coming years;
Thou think'st of sorrow, pain, and loneliness,
And the bright world seems but a vale of tears.
Go and tell Jesus, — he will say to thee,
I thy good Shepherd am; O, trust in me!

Go and tell Jesus; so shall he be thine,
And sweetly will he come and dwell with thee.
Tell *all* to Jesus; so shalt thou be his,
His through all time and all eternity.
Saviour, I come; O, teach me how to pray!
Thou only canst, my life, my truth, my way.

CHRIST'S DISCIPLINE.

"Nevertheless, afterward it yieldeth the peaceable fruit of righteousness unto them which are exercised thereby." — *Heb.* xii. 11.

O Saviour! whose mercy, severe in its kindness,
  Has chastened my wanderings and guided my way,
Adored be the power which illumined my blindness
  And weaned me from phantoms that smiled to betray.

Enchanted with all that was dazzling and fair
  I followed the rainbow, I caught at the toy,
And still in displeasure thy goodness was there,
  Disappointing the hope and defeating the joy.

The blossom blushed bright, — but a worm was below;
  The moonlight shone fair, — there was blight in the beam;

Sweet whispered the breeze, but it whispered of woe,
    And bitterness flowed in the soft-flowing stream.

So, cured of my folly, but cured but in part,
    I turned to the refuge thy pity displayed;
But still did this eager and credulous heart
    Weave visions of joy that bloomed but to fade.

I thought that the course of the pilgrim to heaven
    Would be bright as the sun, and glad as the morn;
Thou show'dst me the path, — it was dark and uneven,
    All rugged with rock and all tangled with thorn.

I dreamed of celestial rewards and renown,
    I grasped at the triumph which blesses the brave;
I asked for the palm-branch, the robe, and the crown,
    I asked, and thou show'dst me a cross and a grave.

Subdued and instructed, at length, to thy will
  My hopes and my longings I fain would resign ;
O, give me the heart that can wait and be still,
  Nor know of a wish or a pleasure but thine !

There are mansions exempted from sin and from woe,
  But they stand in a region by mortals untrod.
There are rivers of joy, but they roll not below ;
  There is rest, but it dwells in the presence of God.

THE BORDER-LAND.

"For the Lord thy God bringeth thee into a good land, a land of brook water, of fountains and depths that spring out of valleys and hills." — I viii. 7.

I have been to a land, a Border-land,
   Where there was but a strange, dim light,
Where shadows and dreams in a spectral band
   Seemed real to the aching sight.
I scarce bethought me how there I came,
   Or if thence I should pass again;
Its morning and light were marked by the flight
   Or coming of woe and pain.

But I saw from this land, this Border-land,
   With mountain ridges hoar,
That they looked across to a wondrous strand,
   A bright and unearthly shore.
Then I turned me to Him, "the Crucified,"
   In most humble faith and prayer,

Who had ransomed with blood my sinful soul,
    For I thought he would call me there.

Yet nay; for a while in the Border-land
    He bade me in patience stay,
And gather rich fruits with a trembling hand,
    Whilst he cheered its glooms away.
He has led me amid those shadows dim
    And shown that bright world so near,
To teach me that earnest trust in Him
    Is the one thing needful here.

NOT UNCLOTHED, BUT CLOTHED UPON.

"For we that are in this tabernacle do groan, being burdened; not for that we would be unclothed, but clothed upon, that mortality might be swallowed up of life." — 2 *Cor.* v. 4.

In health, O Lord, and prosperous days,
When worldly wealth, or worldly praise,
When worldly thoughts have filled our heart,
We would not from the body part ; —
And then the very thought is loathed,
That we must be by death unclothed.

In sickness, sorrow, or in shame,
We fain would quit this mortal frame ;
But thus to shrink from toil and pain, —
This is not longing for thy reign ;
Brought low, we only seek to be
Unclothed, — not clothed upon by thee.

O, rather help us as we ought
To feel what thine apostle taught, —
That not for aye we seek to wear
This form of clay, corruption's heir;
Nor yet, impatient, ask alone
To be unclothed, but clothed upon.

O blessed Lord! whose merits dress
Thy saints in robes of righteousness;
Through whom, for us, eternal stands
That heavenly house, not made with hands, —
When this frail dwelling sets us free,
Quench thou, in life, mortality.

FRIENDSHIP WITH CHRIST.

"Nevertheless, I am continually with thee; thou hast holden me by my right hand." — *Ps.* lxxiii. 23.

When, in the hours of lonely woe,
I give my sorrows leave to flow,
And anxious fear and dark distrust
Weigh down my spirit to the dust;
When not e'en friendship's gentle aid
Can heal the wounds the world has made;
O, this shall check each rising sigh, —
Thou, Saviour, art for ever nigh.

Jesus! in whom, but thee above,
Can I repose my trust, my love?
And shall an earthly object be
Loved, in comparison with thee?
Thy counsels and upholding care

My safety and my comfort are;
Thou, Lord, shalt guide me all my days,
Till glory crown the work of grace.

My flesh is hastening to decay, —
Soon shall the world have passed away, —
And what can mortal friends avail,
When heart and strength and flesh shall fail!
But, O, be thou, my Saviour. nigh,
And I will triumph while I die;
My strength, my portion, is divine,
And Jesus is for ever mine!

CHRIST'S CARE.

"Master, carest thou not that we perish?" — *Mark* iv. 38

Such was the disciples' cry,
When the crested waves beat high,
And the heavens above were dark,
O'er the tempest-driven bark.

Such, O Lord, in trial's hour,
When afflictions round us lower,
Now, on life's tempestuous sea,
Our complaining cry to thee.

But thou didst not, though upbraided,
Leave thy followers then unaided;
Prompt to succor, swift to save,
Thou rebukedst wind and wave.

At the word which spoke thy will,
Every stormy wind was still;
At thy voice the waves subsided,
And in gentlest murmurs glided.

Though their faith, too often frail,
In thy power divine might fail;
Though thou mightst reprove their fear,
Still thy saving arm was near.

Thus, O Lord, on us look down,
When above us clouds may frown;
Tossing on a stormy sea,
Helpless, hopeless, but for thee.

Should we deem ourselves forgot,
Let thy mercies fail us not;
But, in doubt's distrustful hour,
Magnify thy love and power.

LOOKING UNTO JESUS.

Heb. xii. 2.

Thou, who didst stoop below,
To drain the cups of woe,
Wearing the form of frail mortality,
Thy blessèd labors done,
Thy crown of victory won,
Hast passed from earth, — passed to thy home on high

Man may no longer trace,
In thy celestial face,
The image of the bright, the viewless One;
Nor may thy servants hear,
Save with faith's raptured ear,
Thy voice of tenderness, God's holy Son!

HYMNS.

Our eyes behold thee not;
Yet hast thou not forgot
Those who have placed their hope, their trust, in thee;
Before thy Father's face
Thou hast prepared a place,
That where thou art, there they may also be.

It was no path of flowers,
Through this dark world of ours,
Belovèd of the Father, thou didst tread;
And shall we in dismay
Shrink from the narrow way,
When clouds and darkness are around it spread?

O Thou, who art our life,
Be with us through the strife!
Was not thy head by earth's fierce tempests bowed?
Raise thou our eyes above,
To see a Father's love
Beam, like the bow of promise, through the cloud.

Even through the awful gloom,
Which hovers o'er the tomb,
That light of love our guiding star shall be;
Our spirits shall not dread
The shadowy way to tread,
Friend, Guardian, Saviour, which doth lead to thee.

LOVE TO CHRIST.

"Who shall separate us from the love of Christ?" — *Rom.* viii. 25.

Though sorrows rise and dangers roll
In waves of darkness o'er my soul;
Though friends are false and love decays
And few and evil are my days;
Though conscience, fiercest of my foes,
Swells with remembered guilt my woes;
Yet even in nature's utmost ill,
I love thee, Lord! I love thee still!

Though Sinai's curse, in thunder dread,
Peals o'er mine unprotected head,
And memory points, with busy pain,
To grace and mercy given in vain,
Till nature, shrinking in the strife,
Would fly to hell to 'scape from life;
Though every thought has power to kill,
I love thee, Lord! I love thee still!

O, by the pangs thyself hast borne,
The ruffian's blow, the tyrant's scorn;
By Sinai's curse, whose dreadful doom
Was buried in thy guiltless tomb;
By these my pangs, whose healing smart
Thy grace has planted in my heart, —
I know, I feel, thy bounteous will,
Thou lov'st me, Lord! Thou lov'st me still!

PATIENCE.

"But let patience have her perfect work." — *James* i. 4.

O thou, to wisdom near allied,
A female virtue void of pride,
 Though more, a grace, divine;
Virtue or grace, whiche'er thou art,
The frequent sigh that rends my heart
 Proves that thou art not mine.

Though here no furious passion sways,
Too oft a starting tear betrays
 A pang that should not be;
Though no resentment holds her seat,
Too apt the unequal pulse to beat,
 Sweet Patience, not to thee.

Could reason and her powers of thought
Calm the quick sense to anguish brough*
    Soon would the tumult cease;
Pride might control the wayward will,
And bid the rising storm be still,
    But vainly whispers peace.

'T is thine, O Patience, to endure
The ills which reason cannot cure,
    The trespass unforgiven,
The cold neglect, the taunting sneer;
Stingless the insult meets his ear,
    Whose eyes are fixed on heaven.

Fixed on that dear availing sign,
Where once thy suffering Lord and mine
    Bowed his meek head and died;
Vain follower of thy suffering Lord,
Think of his life, his death record,
    And blush that e'er you sighed.

CHASTISEMENT.

" As many as I love, I rebuke and chasten." — Rev. iii. 19.

Glory to the righteous God, —
   Righteous, yet benign to me!
Still, in his paternal rod,
   His paternal love I see;
Let him tenderly chastise,
   Let him graciously reprove, —
Father, all within me cries,
   "All thy ways are truth and love."

Humbled in the lowest deep,
   Thee I for my sufferings bless;
Think of all thy love, and weep
   For my own unfaithfulness:
I have most rebellious been,
   Thou hast laid thy hand on me,
Kindly visited my sin,
   Scourged the wanderer back to thee.

Taught obedience to my God,
  By the things I have endured,
Meekly now I kiss the rod,
  Wounded by that rod and cured;
Good for me the grief and pain,
  Let me but thy grace adore,
Keep the pardon I regain,
  Stand in awe, and sin no more.

"GOD IS LOVE."

1 John iv. 8.

'T is sweet when cloudless suns arise,
  As through the vale we move;
But, O! more sweet to recognize,
Through dreary nights and starless skies,
  The smiling face of Love!

I hail the breeze that, soft and clear,
    Wafts influence from above;
But chief the storm delighted hear,
While breathes o'er faith's attentive ear
    The whispering voice of Love!

When health invigorates the frame,
    Let joy the bliss improve;
But torturing pain, and fever's flame,
With teaching power alike proclaim
    The tender hand of Love!

Thou canst not weep, frail child of clay,
    Such blessings taught to prove;
Each cloud that dims thy upward way
Shall more endear the glorious day,
    That gilds the land of Love!

BOWRING.

"O, BRING ME OUT OF MY DISTRESSES!"

Psalm xxv. 17.

Thou man of griefs, remember me,
   Who never canst thyself forget, —
Thy last mysterious agony,
   Thy fainting pangs and bloody sweat;
When, wrestling in the strength of prayer,
   Thy spirit sunk beneath its load;
Thy feeble flesh abhorred to bear
   The wrath of an Almighty God.

Father! if I may call thee so,
   Regard my fearful heart's desire;
Remove this load of guilty woe,
   Nor let me in my sins expire:
I tremble lest the wrath divine,
   Which bruises now my sinful soul,
Should bruise this wretched soul of mine
   Long as eternal ages roll.

To thee my last distress I bring;
   The heightened fear of death I find;
The tyrant, brandishing his sting,
   Appears, and hell is close behind!
I deprecate that death alone,
   That endless banishment from thee!
O, save, and give me to thy Son,
   Who trembled, wept, and bled for me!
WESLEY.

GOD APPOINTS.

"But the very hairs of your head are all numbered." — *Matt.* x. 30.

Is thy path lonely ? fear it not, for He
Who marks the sparrow's fall is guarding thee ;
And not a star shines o'er thy head by night,
But He doth know that it will meet thy sight,
And not a joy can beautify thy lot,
But tells thee still that thou art unforgot.
Nay, not a grief can darken or surprise,
Dwell in thy heart, or dim with tears thine eyes,
But it is sent in mercy and in love,
To bid thy helplessness seek strength above.

GLORY TO GOD.

"Thou art worthy, O Lord, to receive glory." — *Rev.* iv. 11.

While I walk life's thorny road,
Path of pain, by Jesus trod,
Lead me from temptation's snare,
Be my shield where perils are;
And my thankful song shall be,
   Gloria tibi, Domine!

When the weary race is past,
When the goal is reached at last;
When sad heart and aching head
In the grave find peaceful bed;
When the ransomed soul shall rise
All exultant to the skies;
Still my joyful song shall be,
   Gloria tibi, Domine!

"A LIVING SACRIFICE."

Rom. xii. 1.

FATHER, Son, and Holy Ghost,
    One in three, and three in one,
As by the celestial host,
    Let thy will on earth be done:
Praise by all to thee be given,
Glorious Lord of earth and heaven!

Vilest of the fallen race,
    Lo! I answer to thy call:
Meanest vessel of thy grace, —
    Grace divinely free for all, —
Lo! I come to do thy will,
All thy counsel to fulfil.

If so poor a worm as I
  May to thy great glory live,
All my actions sanctify,
  All my words and thoughts receive:
Claim me for thy service, claim
All I have and all I am.

Take my soul's and body's powers,
  Take my memory, mind, and will;
All my goods and all my hours,
  All I know, and all I feel;
All I think, and speak, and do:
Take my heart, — but make it new!

Now, O God, thine own I am:
  Now I give thee back thine own, —
Freedom, friends, and health, and fame,
  Consecrate to thee alone:
Thine I live, thrice happy I, —
Happier still, when thine I die.

C. Wesley.

BELIEVING IN HOPE.

"Who against hope believed in hope." — Rom. iv. 18.

Who is the weak believer, who
Doth still his weary way pursue;
Inspired with true religious fear,
And following Christ with heart sincere?
Obedient to thy Saviour's voice,
Yet canst thou not in him rejoice,
Nor taste the comforts of his grace,
Nor find a God who hides his face.

Jesus is vanished from thy sight, —
No glimpse of bliss or gleam of light,
To cheer thee in the desert way,
Or promise a return of day.
No evidence of things unseen,
But wars without and fears within, —
No witness of thy sins forgiven,
No ray of hope on this side heaven!

Poor, tempted soul, what canst thou do?
Hope against hope, that God is true:
His nature in his name confess,
His wisdom, power, and righteousness.
The Lord, whom now thou canst not see,
Whate'er he is, he is *for* thee:
Expect, and thou shalt surely prove,
That God in Christ is perfect love.

WESLEY.

"WATCH YE."

1 *Cor.* xvi. 13.

When summer decks thy path with flowers,
   And pleasure's smile is sweetest;
When not a cloud above thee lowers,
And sunshine leads thy happy hours,
   Thy happiest and thy fleetest;
O, watch thou, then, lest pleasure's smile
Thy spirit of its hope beguile!

When round thee gathering storms are nigh,
    And grief thy days hath shaded ;
When earthly joys but bloom to die,
And tears suffuse thy weeping eye,
    And hope's bright bow hath faded ;
O, watch thou, then, lest anxious care
Invade thy heart, and rankle there !

Through all life's scenes, through weal and woe,
    Through days of mirth and sadness;
Where'er thy wandering footsteps go, —
O, think how transient here below
    Thy sorrow and thy gladness !
And watch thou always, lest thou stray
From Him who points the heavenward way.

BETHESDA.

John v. 2 - 9.

Around Bethesda's healing wave,
    Waiting to hear the rustling wing
Which spoke the angel nigh, who gave
    Its virtues to that holy spring, —
With earnest, fixèd solitude,
Were seen the afflicted multitude.

Among them there was one, whose eye
    Had often seen the waters stirred,
Whose heart had often heaved the sigh,
    The bitter sigh of hope deferred,
Beholding, while he suffered on,
The healing virtue given, — and gone.

No power had he ; no friendly aid
    To him its timely succor brought ;
But while his coming he delayed,
    Another won the boon he sought ; —
Until the Saviour's love was shown,
Which healed him by a word alone !

Had they who watched and waited there
    Been conscious who was passing by,
With what unceasing, anxious care
    Would they have sought his pitying eye ;
And craved, with fervency of soul,
His sovereign power to make them whole.

But habit and tradition swayed
    Their mind to trust to sense alone ;
They only sought the angel's aid ;
    While in their presence stood, unknown,
A greater, mightier far, than he, —
With power from grief and pain to free.

Bethesda's pool has lost its power;
　No angel by his glad descent
Dispenses that diviner dower,
　Which with its healing waters went;
But He, whose word surpassed its wave,
Is still omnipotent to save.

BARTON.

MIZPAH.

"The Lord watch between me and thee, when we are absent one from another." — *Gen.* xxxi. 49.

When friend from friend is parting,
   And in each speaking eye
The silent tears are starting,
   To tell what words deny;
How could we bear the heavy load
   Of such heart-agony,
Could we not cast it all, our God,
   Our gracious God, on thee?
And feel that thou kind watch will keep
   When we are far away;
That thou wilt soothe us when we weep,
   And hear us when we pray.

Yet oft these hearts will whisper,
  That better 't would betide,
If we were near the friends we love,
  And watching by their side;
But sure thou 'lt love them dearer, Lord,
  For trusting thee alone;
And sure thou wilt draw nearer, Lord,
  The further we are gone.
Then why be sad? since thou wilt keep
  Watch o'er them day by day;
Since thou wilt soothe *them* when they weep,
  And hear *us* when we pray.

O for that bright and happy land,
  Where, far amid the blest,
' The wicked cease from troubling, and
  The weary are at rest."
Where friends are never parted,
  Once met around thy throne;

And none are broken-hearted,
  Since all, with thee, are one !
Yet, O, till then, watch o'er us keep,
  While far from thee away ;
And soothe us, Lord, oft as we weep,
  And hear us when we pray.
                    MONSELL.

THE BIBLE.

"The law of thy mouth is better unto me than thousands of gold and
lver."— *Ps.* cxix. 72.

PRECIOUS Bible ! what a treasure
  Does the word of God afford !
All I want for life or pleasure,
  Food and medicine, shield and sword :
Let the world account me poor,
Having this I need no more.

Food, to which the world 's a stranger,
    Here my hungry soul enjoys ;
Of excess there is no danger,
    Though it fills, it never cloys :
On a dying Christ I feed,
He is meat and drink indeed.

When my faith is faint and sickly,
    Or when Satan wounds my mind,
Cordials to revive me quickly,
    Healing medicines, here I find :
To the promises I flee,
Each affords a remedy.

In the hour of dark temptation,
    Satan cannot make me yield,
For the word of consolation
    Is to me a mighty shield :
While the Scripture truths **are sure,**
From his malice I 'm secure.

Shall I envy, then, the miser,
    Doating on his golden store?
Sure I am, or should be, wiser;
    I am rich, 't is he is poor:
Jesus gives me in his word
Food and medicine, shield and sword.

NEWTON.

HOME.

"Then the disciples went away unto their own home." — *John* xx. 10.

Where burns the fireside brightest
    Cheering the social breast?
Where beats the fond heart lightest,
    Its humble hopes possessed?
Where is the hour of sadness
    With meek-eyed patience borne?

Worth more than those of gladness,
  Which mirth's gay cheeks adorn!
Pleasure is marked by fleetness,
  To those who ever roam;
While grief itself has sweetness,
        At home, — sweet home!

There blend the ties that strengthen
  Our hearts in hours of grief, —
The silver links that lengthen
  Joy's visits, when most brief:
There, eyes, in all their splendor,
  Are vocal to the heart;
And glances, bright and tender,
  Fresh eloquence impart:
Then, dost thou sigh for pleasure?
  O, do not widely roam;
But seek that hidden treasure
        At home, — sweet home!

Does pure religion charm thee
    Far more than aught below?
Wouldst thou that she should arm thee
    Against the hour of woe?
Her dwelling is not only
    In temples built for prayer;
For home itself is lonely,
    Unless her smiles be there;
Wherever we may wander,
    'T is all in vain we roam,
If worshipless her altar
        At home, — sweet home!
                    BARTON.

HOUSEHOLD HARMONY.

"Behold, how good and how pleasant it is for brethren to dwell together in unity!" — *Ps.* cxxxiii. 1.

O, SWEET as vernal dews, that fill
The closing buds on Zion's hill,

When evening clouds draw thither.
So sweet, so heavenly, 't is to see
The members of one family
   Live peacefully together!

The children, like the lily flowers,
On which descend the sun and showers,
   Their hues of beauty blending,—
The parents, like the willow boughs,
On which the lovely foliage grows,
   Their friendly shade extending.

But leaves the greenest will decay,
And flowers the brightest fade away,
   When autumn winds are sweeping,
And be the household e'er so fair,
The hand of death will soon be there,
   And turn the scene to weeping!

Yet leaves again will clothe the trees,
And lilies wave beneath the breeze,
    When spring comes smiling hither;
And friends, who parted at the tomb,
May yet renew their loveliest bloom,
    And meet in heaven together!

Knox.

THE NAME OF JESUS.

"And thou shalt call his name Jesus; for he shall save his people from their sins." — *Matt.* i. 21.

How sweet the name of Jesus sounds
    In a believer's ear!
It soothes his sorrows, heals his wounds,
    And drives away his fear.

It makes the wounded spirit whole,
    And calms the troubled breast;
'T is manna to the hungry soul
    And to the weary, rest.

Dear name! the rock on which I build,
    My shield and hiding-place,
My never-failing treasury, filled
    With boundless stores of grace!

By thee my prayers acceptance gain,
    Although with sin defiled
Satan accuses me in vain,
    And I am owned a child.

Jesus! my Shepherd, Husband, **Friend**,
    My Prophet, Priest, and King,
My Lord, my Life, my Way, my **End**!
    Accept the praise I bring.

Weak is the effort of my heart,
   And cold my warmest thought;
But when I see thee as thou art,
   I 'll praise thee as I ought.

Till then I would thy love proclaim,
   With every fleeting breath;
And may the music of thy name
   Refresh my soul in death.

Newton.

THE COURTS OF THE LORD

Psa'm lxxxiv.

Pleasant are thy courts above,
In the land of light and love;
Pleasant are thy courts below,
In this land of sin and woe.
O, my spirit longs and faints
For the converse of thy saints;
For the brightness of thy face,
King of Glory, God of grace!

Happy birds, that sing and fly
Round thy altars, O Most High!
Happier souls, that find a rest
In a Heavenly Father's breast!
Like the wandering dove, that found
No repose on earth around,
They can to their ark repair,
And enjoy it ever there.

Happy souls! their praises flow
Even in this vale of woe,
Waters in the desert rise,
Manna feeds them from the skies;
On they go from strength to strength,
Till they reach thy throne at length,
At thy feet adoring fall,
Who hast led them safe through all.

Lord, be mine this prize to win,
Guide me through a world of sin;
Keep me by thy saving grace,
Give me at thy side a place.
Sun and shield alike thou art,
Guide and guard my erring heart;
Grace and glory flow from thee,
Shower, O, shower them, Lord, on me!
LYTE.

SICKNESS ON THE SABBATH.

"When shall I come and appear before God?" — *Ps.* xlii. 2.

I HEAR the bells, I see them go,
   I may not join the throng
Of faithful Christians here below,
   Nor hear the grateful song,
Which in those sacred walls they raise
Unto our blessed Redeemer's praise.

Dare I repine, or think it hard,
   By sickness and by pain,
That I should be so long debarred
   Treading those courts again?
O, no! it is my Father's will;
'T is his command; my heart, be still!

For well I know his love is raised
   Beyond what we can feel;

HYMNS.

His word is sure, his truth engaged
    The weak to raise and heal.
I know that his almighty power
Surrounds and guards me every hour.

In weakness, Lord, be thou my strength;
    And when it is thy will
In health to raise me up at length,
    Make me to praise thee still;
And feel, that thy afflicting rod
Has drawn me nearer to my God.

And when life's weary path is trod,
    Its fleeting shadows past;
May I repose on thee, my God,
    In perfect peace, at last!
Then shall I know, then shall I see,
That all has worked for good to me.

THE FOUNTAIN OPENED.

"In that day there shall be a fountain opened to the house of David, and to the inhabitants of Jerusalem, for sin and for uncleanness." — *Zech.* xiii. 1.

There is a fountain filled with blood,
   Drawn from Immanuel's veins,
And sinners, plunged beneath that flood,
   Lose all their guilty stains.

The dying thief rejoiced to see
   That fountain in his day;
And there have I, as vile as he,
   Washed all my sins away.

Dear, dying Lamb! thy precious **blood**
   Shall never lose its power,
Till all the ransomed Church **of God**
   Be saved, to sin no more.

E'er since, by faith, I saw the stream
   Thy flowing wounds supply,
Redeeming love has been my theme,
   And shall be till I die.

Then, in a nobler, sweeter song,
   I 'll sing thy power to save;
When this poor, lisping, stammering tongue
   Lies silent in the grave.

Lord, I believe thou hast prepared
   (Unworthy though I be)
For me a blood-bought, free reward,
   A golden harp for me.

'T is strung and tuned for endless years,
   And formed by power divine,
To sound in God the Father's ears
   No other name but thine.

COWPER.

DETAINED FROM THE SANCTUARY.

"For I had gone with the multitude; I went with them to the house of God with the voice of joy and praise, with a multitude that kept holy day." — *Ps* xlii. 4.

Sweet Sabbath bells! I love your voice,—
   You call me to the house of prayer;
Oft have you made my heart rejoice,
   When I have gone to worship there.

But now, a prisoner of the Lord,
   His hand forbids, I cannot go;
Yet may I here his love record,
   And here the sweets of worship know.

Each place alike is holy ground,
   Where prayer from humble souls is **poured**,
Where praise awakes its silver sound,
   Or God is silently adored.

HYMNS.

His sanctuary is the heart, —
   There, with the contrite, will he rest;
Lord, come, a Sabbath frame impart,
   And make thy temple in my breast.

SLEEP.

"So he giveth his beloved sleep." — *Ps.* cxxvii. 2.

Of all the thoughts of God, that are
Borne inward unto souls afar,
   Along the Psalmist's music deep, —
     Now tell me if that any is
     For gift or grace surpassing this, —
"He giveth his beloved sleep"?

What would we give to *our* beloved ?
The hero's heart, to be unmoved, —
  The poet's star-tuned harp, to sweep, —
    The senate's shout for patriot vows, —
    The monarch's crown to light the brows?
" He giveth his beloved sleep."

What do we give to our beloved ?
A little faith, all undisproved, —
  A little dust, to overweep, —
    And bitter memories, to make
    The whole earth blasted for our sake!
" He giveth his beloved sleep."

'Sleep soft, beloved!" we sometimes say;
But have no tune to charm away
  Sad dreams, that through the eyelids creep·
    But never doleful dream again
    Shall break the happy slumber, when
" He giveth his beloved sleep."

HYMNS.

O earth, so full of dreamy noises!
O men, with wailing in your voices!
  O delvèd gold, the wailer's heap!
    O strife, O curse, that o'er it fall!
    God makes a silence through you all,
  And " giveth his beloved sleep."

His dews drop mutely on the hill, —
His cloud above it saileth still, —
  Though on its slope men toil and reap;
    More softly than the dew is shed,
    Or cloud is floated overhead,
  " He giveth his beloved sleep."

Yea! men may wonder, while they scan
A living, thinking, feeling man,
  In such a rest his heart to keep;
    But angels say, — and through the word,
    I ween, their blessed smile is heard, —
  " He giveth his beloved sleep."

For me, my heart, that erst did go
Most like a tired child at a show,
   That sees, through tears, the juggler's leap,
    Would now its wearied vision close,
    And childlike on His love repose,
Who " giveth his beloved sleep."

And friends, dear friends! when it shall be
That this low breath is gone from me, —
   When round my bier ye come to weep, —
    Let one, most loving of you all,
    Say, — " Not a tear must o'er her fall, —
He giveth his beloved sleep."
                   ELIZABETH BARRETT BROWNING.

"IF CHRIST IS MINE."

Cant. ii. 16.

" If Christ is mine," then all is mine,
   And more than angels know ;
Both present things, and things to come,
   And grace and glory, too.

" If he is mine," then, though he frown,
   He never will forsake ;
His chastisements all work for good,
   And but his love bespeak.

" If he is mine," I need not fear
   The rage of earth and hell ;
He will support my feeble frame,
   And all their power repel.

"If he is mine," let friends forsake,
    And earthly comforts flee;
He, the dispenser of all good,
    Is more than these to me.

"If he is mine," I'll fearless pass
    Through death's tremendous vale;
He'll be my comfort and my stay,
    When heart and flesh shall fail.

Let Christ assure me "he is mine,"
    I nothing want beside;
My soul shall at the fountain live,
    When all the streams are dried.

BEDDOME.

EVENING LITANY.

"Let my prayer be set forth before thee as incense; and the lifting up of my hands as the evening sacrifice." — *Ps.* cxli. 2.

FATHER! by thy love and power,
Comes again the evening hour;
Light has vanished, labors cease,
Weary creatures rest in peace.
Thou, whose genial dews distil
   On the lowliest weed that grows,
Father! guard our couch from ill,
   Lull thy children to repose;
We to thee ourselves resign,
Let our latest thoughts be thine.

Saviour! to thy Father bear
This, our feeble evening prayer;

Thou hast seen how oft, to-day,
We, like sheep, have gone astray;
Worldly thoughts, and thoughts of pride,
    Wishes to thy cross untrue;
Secret faults, and undescribed,
    Meet thy spirit-piercing view;
Blessed Saviour! yet, through thee,
Pray that these may pardoned be.

Holy Spirit! breath of balm!
Fall on us in evening's calm;
Yet awhile, before we sleep,
We with thee will vigils keep:
Lead us on our sins to muse,
    Give us truest penitence;
Then the love of God infuse,
    Breathing humble confidence;
Melt our spirits, mould our will,—
Soften, strengthen, comfort still.

Blessed Trinity! be near,
Through the hours of darkness drear;
When the help of man is far,
Ye more clearly present are;—
Father, Son, and Holy Ghost,
  Watch o'er our defenceless head;
Let your angels, guardian host,
  Keep all evil from our bed,
Till the flood of morning rays
Wake us to a song of praise.

EVENING HYMN.

"Man goeth forth unto his work and to his labor until the evening."—
Ps. civ. 23.

The gaudy day is dying!
The hours of evening, flying,
    Chase household cares away;
Awhile soft twilight lingers,
Till night with dewy fingers
    Shall close the weary eye of day.

O, let us, ere we slumber,
Heaven's bounties try to number,
    Too great for tongue to tell;
Our grateful hearts confessing,
With each recounted blessing,
    That God has ordered all things well.

No fears disturb us sleeping,
Our souls are in thy keeping,
    Our hearts repose on thee;
For thou wilt ne'er forsake us,
Whether the dawn awake us
    Here, or in blest eternity.

Lord! 't is thy hand that guides us,
And with all good provides us,
    In this our pilgrimage,
O, be our praise unceasing,
Our love each day increasing
    To life's remote and latest stage!

RINCK

EVENING TIME.

"It shall come to pass, that at evening there shall be light." — *Zech.* xiv. 7

At evening time, let there be light;
   Life's little day draws near its close;
Around me fall the shades of night,
   The night of death, the grave's repose;
   To crown my joys, to end my woes,
At evening time, let there be light.

At evening time, let there be light;
   Stormy and dark hath been my day;
Yet rose the morn divinely bright, —
   Dews, birds, and blossoms cheered the way;
   O for one sweet, one parting ray! —
At evening time, let there be light.

At evening time, there *shall* be light,
    For God hath spoken, — it must be;
Fear, doubt, and anguish take their flight,
    His glory now is risen on me;
    Mine eyes shall his salvation see;
'T is evening time, — and there *is* light.
Montgomery.

MIDNIGHT HYMN.

"At midnight I will rise to give thanks unto thee, because of thy righteous judgments." — *Ps.* cxix. 62.

In the mid silence of the voiceless night,
When, chased by airy dreams, the slumbers flee;
Whom, in the darkness, doth my spirit seek,
    O God, but thee?

And, if there be a weight upon my breast,
Some vague impression of the day foregone,
Scarce knowing what it is, I fly to thee,
    And lay it down.

Or, if it be the heaviness that comes
In token of anticipated ill,
My bosom takes no heed of what it is,
    Since 't is thy will.

For, O, in spite of past or present care,
Or any thing beside, — how joyfully
Passes that silent, solitary hour,
  My God, with thee!

More tranquil than the stillness of the night,
More peaceful than the silence of that hour,
More blest than any thing, my bosom lies
  Beneath thy power.

For, what is there on earth, that I desire,
Of all that it can give, or take from me?
Or whom, in heaven, doth my spirit seek,
  O God, but thee?

NIGHT.

"The morning cometh, and also the night." — *Isa.* xxi. 12.

Night is the time to muse;
  Then, from the eye, the soul
Takes flight; and, with expanded views,
  Beyond the starry pole,
Descries, athwart the abyss of night,
The dawn of uncreated light.

Night is the time to pray;
  Our Saviour oft withdrew
To desert mountains far away;
  So will his followers do,
Steal from the throng to haunts untrod,
And hold communion there with God.

Night is the time for death;
　When all around is peace,
Calmly to yield the weary breath,
　From sin and suffering cease;
Think of heaven's bliss, and give the sign
To parting friends, — such death be mine.
　　　　　　　　MONTGOMERY.

MORNING.

"The morning cometh, and also the night." — *Isa.* xxi. 12.

Morn is the time to think,
　While thoughts are fresh and free,
Of life, just balanced on the brink
　Of dark eternity;
And ask our souls, if they are meet
To stand before the judgment-seat.

Morn is the time to die, —
  Just at the dawn of day,
When stars are fading in the sky,
  To fade, like them, away;
But lost in light more brilliant far,
Than ever merged the morning star.

Morn is the time to rise,
  The resurrection morn,
Upspringing to the glorious skies,
  On new-found pinions borne,
To meet a Saviour's smile divine, —
Be such ecstatic rising mine.

I. L. GRAY.

HYMNS.

AUTUMNAL HYMN.

"And we all do fade as a leaf." —*Isa.* lxiv. 6.

The leaves around me falling,
   Are preaching of decay;
The hollow winds are calling,
   "Come, pilgrim, come away!"
The day, in night declining,
   Says, I must, too, decline;
The year, its life resigning, —
   Its lot foreshadows mine.

The light my path surrounding,
   The loves, to which I cling,
The hopes within me bounding,
   The joys, that round me wing, —
All melt, like stars of even,
   Before the morning's ray, —
Pass upward into heaven,
   And chide at my delay.

The friends, gone there before me,
   Are calling from on high,
And joyous angels o'er me,
   Tempt sweetly to the sky.
" Why wait, they say, " and wither,
   'Mid scenes of death and sin?
O, rise to glory, hither,
   And find true life begin!"

I hear the invitation,
   And fain would rise and come, —
A sinner to salvation;
   An exile to his home:
But, while I here must linger,
   Thus, thus let all I see
Point on, with faithful finger
   To heaven, O Lord, and thee.

LYTE.

FOR MY MOTHER.

"Despise not thy mother when she is old." — *Prov.* xxiii. 22.

O, how soft that bed must be,
   Made in sickness, Lord, by thee!
And that rest, how calm, how sweet,
   Where Jesus and the sufferer meet!

It was the good Physician now
   Soothed thy cheek and chafed thy brow;
Whispering, as he raised thy head, —
   " It is I, be not afraid."

God of glory, God of grace,
   Hear from heaven, thy dwelling-place;
Hear, in mercy, and forgive,
   Bid thy child believe, and live.

Bless her, and she shall be blest,
    Soothe her, and she shall have rest ; .
Fix her heart, her hopes, above,
    Love her, Lord, for thou art love.

THE AGED.

"Now, also, when I am old and gray-headed, O God, forsake me not; until I have showed thy strength unto this generation, and thy power to every one that is to come." — *Ps.* lxxi. 18.

With years oppressed, with sorrows worn,
Dejected, harassed, sick, forlorn,
    To thee, O God, I pray ;
To thee my withered hands arise,
To thee I lift these failing eyes,
    O, cast me not away !

HYMNS.

Thy mercy heard my infant prayer,
Thy love, with all a mother's care,
   Sustained my childish days,
Thy goodness watched my ripening youth,
And formed my heart to love thy truth,
   And filled my lips with praise.

O Saviour! has thy grace declined?
Can years affect the Eternal mind?
   Or time its lone decay?
A thousand ages pass thy sight,
And all their long and weary flight
   Is gone like yesterday.

Then, even in age and grief, thy name
Shall still my languid heart inflame,
   And bow my faltering knee.
O, yet this bosom feels the fire,
This trembling hand and drooping lyre
   Have yet a strain for thee.

Yes, broken, tuneless, still, O Lord,
This voice transported shall record
   Thy goodness tried so long:
Till sinking slow, with calm decay,
Its feeble murmurs melt away
   Into a seraph's song.

GRANT.

THE DYING FATHER.

"Leave thy fatherless children, I will preserve them alive; and let thy widows trust in me." — *Jer.* xlix. 11.

O thou faithful God of love!
   Gladly I thy promise plead;
Waiting for my last remove,
   Hastening to the happy dead:
Lo, I cast on thee my care,
Breathe my latest breath in prayer!

Trusting in thy word alone,
   I to thee my children leave;
Call my little ones thine own,
   To them all thy blessings give:
Keep them while on earth they breathe,
Save their souls from endless death.

Whom I to thy grace commend,
    Under thy protection take :
Be her sure, immortal friend ;
    Save her for my Saviour's sake :
Free from sin, from sorrow free,
Let my widow trust in thee.

Father of the fatherless,
    Husband of the widow prove ;
Me and mine vouchsafe to bless,
    Tell me, we shall meet above :
Seal the promise on my heart,
Bid me then in peace depart !

C. WESLEY.

SICKNESS AND HEALING.

"Healing all manner of sickness, and all manner of disease among the people." — *Matt.* iv. 23.

How frail are these bodies of clay!
  How soon all their vigor is lost!
They flourish in beauty to-day, —
  To-morrow they mingle with dust.

So flowers in the morning may rise,
  Unfolding their leaves to the sun;
While the breath of each zephyr that sighs
  May blast them, and soon they are gone.

Afflictions spring not from the ground,
  Diseases our Sovereign obey;
His hand can heal every wound,
  Or fill us with death and dismay.

We lie at thy sovereign control,
  O Lord, in this hour of distress;
Physician of body and soul,
  Send down thy recovering grace.

O, speak, and the dying shall live,
  Jehovah, almighty to save!
At thy voice, e'en the dead shall revive,
  And triumph, at last, o'er the grave.

CONVALESCENCE.

"For indeed he was sick nigh unto death; but God had mercy on him."—
Phil. ii. 27.

All hail! thou lengthener of my days!
Thy still preserving love I praise,
    And thankfully receive
The present of my life restored:
O, may I spend it for thee, Lord,
    And to thy glory live!

No other end of life I 'd know,
Nor would I live one hour below
    But to declare thy praise;
To suffer all thy holy will,
And all thy counsel to fulfil,
    And publish all thy grace.

Wesley

LET HER DEPART.

"While we look not at the things which are seen, but at the things which are not seen." — 2 *Cor.* iv. 18.

HER home is far, O, far away!
　The clear light in her eyes
Hath naught to do with earthly day,
　'T is kindled from the skies.
　　　　Let her depart!

She looks upon the things of earth,
　Even as some gentle star
Seems gazing down on grief or mirth,
　How softly, yet how far!
　　　　Let her depart!

Her spirit's hope, — her bosom's love —
  O, could they mount and fly!
She never sees a wandering dove,
  But for its wings to sigh.
        Let her depart!

She never hears a soft wind bear
  Low music on its way,
But deems it sent from heavenly air,
  For her who cannot stay.
        Let her depart!

Wrapt in a cloud of glorious dreams,
  She breathes and moves alone,
Pining for those bright bowers and streams
  Where her beloved is gone.
        Let her depart!
                HEMANS.

THE SICK CHILD TO HIS MOTHER.

"They desire a better country, that is, an heavenly." — *Heb.* xi. 16.

"I HEAR thee speak of the better land,
Thou call'st its children a happy band;
Mother, O, where is that radiant shore?
Shall we not seek it, and weep no more?
Is it where the flower of the orange blows,
And the fireflies glance through the myrtle boughs?"
   "Not there, not there, my child!"

"Is it where the feathery palm-trees rise,
And the date grows ripe under sunny skies?
Or 'midst the green islands of glittering seas,
Where fragrant forests perfume the breeze,
And strange, bright birds, on their starry wings,
Bear the rich hues of all glorious things?"
   "Not there, not there, my child?"

HYMNS.

"Is it far away, in some region old,
Where the rivers wander o'er sands of gold?
Where the burning rays of the ruby shine,
And the diamond lights up the secret mine,
And the pearl gleams forth from the coral strand?
Is it there, sweet mother, that better land?"
          "Not there, not there, my child!

"Eye hath not seen it, my gentle boy!
Ear hath not heard its deep songs of joy;
Dreams cannot picture a world so fair:
Sorrow and death may not enter there;
Time doth not breathe on its fadeless bloom,
Far beyond the clouds, and beyond the tomb,
          It is there, it is there, my child!"
                    HEMANS.

HYMNS.

THE STRANGER AND HIS FRIEND.

" Ye have done it unto me." — Matt. xxv. 40.

A POOR wayfaring man of grief
   Hath often crossed me in my way,
Who sued so humbly for relief,
   That I could never answer, nay:
I had not power to ask his name,
Whither he went, or whence he came
Yet there was something in his eye
That won my love, I knew not why.

Once, when my scanty meal was spread,
   He entered; not a word he spake.
Just perishing for want of bread,
   I gave him all; he blessed and brake
And ate, — but gave me part again.
Mine was an angel's portion then;
For while I fed with eager haste,
That crust was manna to my taste.

I spied him where a fountain burst
    Clear from the rock ; his strength was gone ;
The heedless water mocked his thirst,
    He heard it, saw it hurrying on.
I ran to raise the sufferer up,
Thrice from the stream he drained my cup,
Dipped and returned it running o'er,—
I drank, and never thirsted more.

'T was night, the floods were out, it blew
    A winter hurricane aloof ;
I heard his voice abroad, and flew
    To bid him welcome to my roof.
I warmed, I clothed, I cheered my guest,
Laid him on my own couch to rest ;
Then made the earth my bed, and seemed
In Eden's garden while I dreamed.

Stripped, wounded, beaten nigh to death,
    I found him by the highway side;
I roused his pulse, brought back his breath,
    Revived his spirits, and supplied
Wine, oil, refreshment; — he was healed; —
I had myself a wound concealed,
But from that hour forgot the smart,
And peace bound up my broken heart.

I saw him next in prison, condemned
    To meet a traitor's doom at morn;
The tide of lying tongues I stemmed,
    And honored him, 'midst shame and scorn.
My friendship's utmost zeal to try,
He asked if I for him would die:
The flesh was weak, my blood ran chill,
But the free spirit cried, — "I will!"

Then in a moment to my view,
   The stranger darted from disguise;
The tokens in his hands I knew,
   My Saviour stood before my eyes!
He spoke, and my poor name he named;
"Of me thou hast not been ashamed,
These deeds shall thy memorial be,
Fear not, — thou didst them unto me."
                                MONTGOMERY.

HYMNS.

"WHY WEEPEST THOU?"

John xx. 13

BROKEN-HEARTED, weep no more!
　Hear what comfort he hath spoken,
Smoking flax who ne'er hath quenched,
　Bruisèd reed who ne'er hath broken: —
　　"Ye who wander here below,
　　Heavy laden as you go!
　　Come, with grief, with sin oppressed,
　　Come to me and be at rest!"

Lamb of Jesus' blood-bought flock,
　Brought again from sin and straying,
Hear the Shepherd's gentle voice, —
　'T is a true and faithful saying: —
　　"Greater love how can there be
　　Than to yield up life for thee?
　　Bought with pain, and tear, and sigh,
　　Turn and live! — why will ye die!"

Broken-hearted, weep no more!
  Far from consolation flying;
He who calls hath felt thy wound,
  Seen thy weeping, heard thy sighing: —
"Bring thy broken heart to me;
  Welcome offering it shall be;
Streaming tears and bursting sighs,
  Mine accepted sacrifice."

JOY IN GOD.

"I will be glad in the Lord." — *Ps.* civ. 34

When morning's first and hallowed ray
  Breaks, with its trembling light,
To chase the pearly dews away,
  Bright tear-drops of the night, —

My heart, O Lord, forgets to rove,
    But rises, gladly free,
On wings of everlasting love,
    And finds its home in thee.

When evening's silent shades descend,
    And nature sinks to rest,
Still, to my Father and my friend
    My wishes are addressed.

Though tears may dim my hours of joy,
    And bid my pleasures flee,
Thou reign'st where grief cannot annoy;
    I will be glad in thee.

And e'en when midnight's solemn gloom,
    Above, around, is spread,
Sweet dreams of everlasting bloom
    Are hovering o'er my head.

I dream of that fair land, O Lord,
  Where all thy saints shall be;
I wake to lean upon thy word,
  And still delight in thee.

THE INVITATION.

"And the Spirit and the bride say, Come. And let him that heareth say, Come. And let him that is athirst, come. And whosoever will, let him take the water of life freely." — *Rev.* xxii. 17.

"Come, who will," — the voice from heaven,
   Like a silver trumpet, calls:
"Come, who will," — the Church hath given
   Back the echo from the walls.

"Come" to rivers ever flowing
   From the high, eternal throne;
"Come," where God, his gifts bestowing,
   In the Church on earth is known.

Heavenly music, — each who listens,
   Longing for his spirit's home,
While his eye with rapture glistens,
   Burns to say, — "I come, I come."

EMPTY AND FLEETING.

"Vanity of vanities, saith the preacher, vanity of vanities; all is vanity." — *Eccl.* i 2.

Ah, how empty, ah, how fleeting,
　Is the *life* of mortal man!
Like the flow of rapid river,
Pausing in its pathway never, —
So our days are flowing, ever.

Ah, how empty, ah, how fleeting,
　Is the *joy* of sighing man!
Transient as a moment's treasure,
Mocking like a shadow's measure, —
So is man's uncertain pleasure.

Ah, how empty, ah, how fleeting,
　Does all human *beauty* seem!
Like the form of a fragile flower,
Withering in an evil hour, —
So is beauty's fading power.

Ah, how empty, ah, how fleeting,
  Is the *honor* of mankind!
Yesterday, the hero hoary
Was the theme of every story, —
Now he lies disrobed of glory.

Ah, how empty, ah, how fleeting,
  Is the *wealth* of eager man!
Fire consumes while he is sleeping,
Floods come on, in fury sweeping, —
Man is left alone, and weeping.

Ah, how empty, ah, how fleeting,
  Are the things of human life!
All things here together taken
May be gone ere we awaken, —
Faith alone remains unshaken.

MICHAEL FRANK.

THE HEAVENLY REST.

" There remaineth, therefore, a rest to the people of God." — Heb. iv. 9

There is an hour of peaceful rest,
 To mourning wanderers given;
There is a joy for souls distressed,
A balm for every wounded breast,—
 'T is found alone in heaven.

There is a soft, a downy bed,
 Far from these shades of even;
A couch for weary mortals spread,
Where they may rest the aching head,
 And find repose,— in heaven.

There is a home for weary souls,
 By sin and sorrow driven;
When tossed on life's tempestuous shoals,
Where storms arise, and ocean rolls,
 And all is drear; — 't is heaven.

There faith lifts up her cheerful eye,
    To brighter prospects given;
And views the tempest passing by,
The evening shadows quickly fly,
    And all serene, in heaven.

There fragrant flowers immortal bloom,
    And joys supreme are given:
There rays divine disperse the gloom:
Beyond the confines of the tomb
    Appears the dawn of heaven.

W. B. Tappan.

HEAVEN ANTICIPATED.

"Knowing in yourselves that ye have in heaven a better and an enduring substance." — *Heb.* x. 34.

Ah! why this disconsolate frame ?
　Though earthly enjoyments decay,
My Jesus is ever the same,
　A sun in the gloomiest day.
Though molten awhile in the fire,
　'T is only the gold to refine ;
And be it my simple desire,
　Though suffering, not to repine.

What can be the pleasure to me,
　Which earth, in its fulness, can boast ?
Delusive, its vanities flee,
　A flash of enjoyment, at most!
And if the Redeemer could part,
　For me, with his throne in the skies,

HYMNS.

Ah! why is so dear to my heart
   What he, in his wisdom, denies?

Though riches to others be given,
   Their corn and their vintage abound;
Yet, if I have treasure in heaven,
   Where should my affections be found?
Why stoop for the glittering sands,
   Which they are so eager to share,
Forgetting those wealthier lands,
   That form my inheritance there?

Dear Jesus, my feelings refine,
   My truant affections recall;
Then, be there no fruit on the vine
   Deserted and empty the stall;
The long-labored olive may die,
   The field may no harvest afford;
But, under the gloomiest sky,
   My soul shall rejoice in the Lord.

Then let the rude tempest assail,
  The blast of adversity blow;
The haven, though distant, I hail,
  Beyond this rough ocean of woe .
When, safe on the beautiful strand,
  I'll smile at the billows, that foam;
Kind angels to hail me to land,
  And Jesus to welcome me home.
                              TAYLOR.

WHAT IS LIFE?

"In the morning it flourisheth, and groweth up; in the evening it is cut own and withereth." — *Ps.* xc. 6.

O, WHAT is life? — 'T is like a flower
  That blossoms, and is gone;
It flourishes its little hour,
  With all its beauty on;
Death comes; and, like a wintry day,
It cuts the lovely flower away.

O, what is life? — 'T is like the bow
　　That glistens in the sky;
We love to see its colors glow,
　　But while we look they die;
Life fails as soon, — to-day 't is here, —
To-morrow it may disappear.

Lord, what is life? — If spent with thee,
　　In humble praise and prayer,
How long or short our life may be,
　　We feel no anxious care;
Though life depart, our joys shall last,
When life and all its joys are past.

TAYLOR.

THE WORLD TO COME.

"But now they desire a better country, that is, an heavenly." — *Heb.* xi. 16.

If all our hopes, and all our fears,
  Were prisoned in life's narrow bound ;
If, travellers through this vale of tears,
  We saw no better world beyond, —
O, what could check the rising sigh,
  What earthly thing could pleasure give?
O, who could venture then to die, —
  Or who could venture then to live ?

Were life a dark and desert moor,
  Where mists and clouds eternal spread
Their gloomy veil behind, before,
  And tempests thunder overhead ;
Where not a sunbeam breaks the gloom,
  And not a floweret smiles beneath, —
Who could exist in such a tomb,
  Who dwell in darkness and in death ?

And such were life, without the ray
  Of our divine religion given;
'T is this that makes our darkness day, —
  'T is this that makes our earth a heaven;
Bright is the golden sun above,
  And beautiful the flowers that bloom;
And all is joy, and all is love,
  Reflected from the world to come.

BOWRING.

THE DYING CHRISTIAN.

"O death, where is thy sting? O grave, where is thy victory?"—1 Cor xv. 55.

" Spirit, leave thine house of clay!
  Lingering dust, resign thy breath!
Spirit, cast thy chains away!
  Dust, be thou dissolved in death!"
Thus the Almighty Saviour speaks,
  While the faithful Christian dies;
Thus the bonds of life he breaks,
  And the ransomed captive flies.

Prisoner, long detained below!
　Prisoner, now with freedom blest!
Welcome, from a world of woe!
　Welcome to a land of rest!"
Thus the choir of angels sing,
　As they bear the soul on high;
While with hallelujahs ring
　All the regions of the sky.

Grave, the guardian of our dust!
　Grave, the treasury of the skies!
Every atom of thy trust
　Rests in hope again to rise!
Hark! the judgment trumpet calls!
　"Soul, rebuild thy house of clay;
Immortality thy walls,
　And *eternity* thy day!"

MONTGOMERY.

SURRENDER AND DEPARTURE

"Into thy hand I commit my spirit: thou hast redeemed me, O Lord God of truth." — *Ps.* xxxi. 5.

God of my life! thy boundless grace
   Chose, pardoned, and adopted me;
My rest, my home, my dwelling-place;
   Father! I come to thee.

Jesus, my hope, my rock, my shield!
   Whose precious blood was shed **for me,**
Into thy hands my soul I yield;
   Saviour! I come to thee.

Spirit of glory and of God!
   Long hast thou deigned my guide to be;
Now be thy comfort sweet bestowed;
   My God! I come to thee.

I come to join that countless host,
    Who praise thy name unceasingly;
Blest Father, Son, and Holy Ghost!
    My God! I come to thee.

WEEP NOT FOR ME.

"What mean ye to weep and to break mine heart?" — *Acts.* xxi. 13.

When the spark of life is waning,
    Weep not for me.
When the languid eye is straining,
    Weep not for me.
When the feeble pulse is ceasing,
Start not at its swift decreasing,
'T is the fettered soul's releasing;
    Weep not for me.

When the pangs of death assail me,
    Weep not for me.
Christ is mine, — he cannot fail me;
    Weep not for me.
Yes, though sin and doubt endeavor
From his love my soul to sever,
Jesus is my strength — for ever!
    Weep not for me.

DABE.

WEEP NOT FOR ME.

"What mean ye to weep and to break mine heart?" — Acts. xxi. 13.

O, WEEP not for me! I can never be blest,
Till my sorrowful spirit in Jesus shall rest
Till this body of sin and of death be destroyed,
And the soul for its glory alone be employed.

O, weep not for me! now my joys will begin;
I shall know the full meaning of ceasing from sin;
I shall know how the saints are made perfect in love,
And be spotless and pure as the angels above.

O, weep not for me! soon my death-pangs will cease,
And this suffering body will slumber in peace;
My soul, even now, is in haste to be gone,
And her robe with the undefiled saints to put on.

O, weep not for me! the glad moment is come,
Which tells me I am now made meet for my home;
My Saviour has willed I should now be removed,
His face to behold, whom unseen I have loved.

O, weep not for me! I can welcome the pains
Which break every bond that my spirit detains;
And ere long, by his own gracious hand, the last tear
Will be wiped from these eyes, which so often weep
    here.

THE RIGHTEOUS IN DEATH.

"Blessed are the dead which die in the Lord, from henceforth." — *Rev* xiv 13.

How blest the righteous when he dies!
 When sinks a weary soul to rest!
How mildly beam the closing eyes!
 How gently heaves the expiring breast!

So fades a summer cloud away;
 So sinks the gale when storms are o'er;
So gently shuts the eye of day;
 So dies a wave along the shore.

A holy quiet reigns around, —
 A calm which life nor death destroys;
And naught disturbs that peace profound,
 Which his unfettered soul enjoys.

Farewell! conflicting hopes and fears,
   Where lights and shades alternate dwell·
How bright the unchanging morn appears!
   Farewell, inconstant world, farewell!

Life's labor done, as sinks the clay,
   Light from its load the spirit flies,
While heaven and earth combine to say,
   "How blest the righteous when he dies!"
BARBAULD.

THE DYING INFANT.

"He shall tell thee what shall become of the child." — 1 Kings xiv. 3.

CEASE here longer to detain me,
   Fondest mother, drowned in woe;
Now thy kind caresses pain me;
   Morn advances, — let me go.

HYMNS.

See yon orient streak appearing!
    Harbinger of endless day;
Hark! a voice, the darkness cheering,
    Calls my new-born soul away!

Lately launched, a trembling stranger,
    On this world's wide, boisterous flood;
Pierced with sorrows, tossed with danger,
    Gladly I return to God.

Now my cries shall cease to grieve thee;
    Now my trembling heart find rest;
Kinder arms than thine receive me,
    Softer pillow than thy breast.

Weep not o'er these eyes that languish,
    Upward turning toward their home:
Raptured they'll forget all anguish,
    While they wait to see thee come.

There, my mother, pleasures centre;
    Weeping, parting, care, or woe
Ne'er our Father's house shall enter: —
    Morn advances, — let me go.

As, through this calm and holy dawning,
    Silent glides my parting breath,
To an everlasting morning,
    Gently close my eyes in death.

Blessings endless, richest blessings,
    Pour their streams upon thy heart!
(Though no language yet possessing,)
    Breathes my spirit ere we part.

Yet to leave thee sorrowing rends me,
    Now again his voice I hear:
Rise! may every grace attend thee,
    Rise! and seek to meet me there.

CECIL.

IMMORTALITY.

"If a man die, shall he live again?" — *Job* xiv. 14.

In the dust I'm doomed to sleep,
  But shall not sleep for ever;
Fear may for a moment weep,
  Christian courage, never.
Years in rapid course shall roll,
  By time's chariot driven,
And my reawakened soul
  Wing its flight to heaven.

What though o'er my mortal tomb
  Clouds and mists be blending?
Sweetest hope shall chase the gloom,
  Hopes to heaven ascending.
These shall be my stay, my trust,
  Ever bright and vernal; —

Life shall blossom out of dust,
Life and joy eternal.

BOWRING.

THE POOR MAN'S DEATH-BED.

"Yet no man remembered that same poor man." — *Eccles.* ix. 15.

TREAD softly! bow the head,
In reverent silence bow!
No passing-bell doth toll,
Yet an immortal soul
    Is passing now.

Stranger! how great soe'er,
With lowly reverence bow!
There's one in that poor shed,
One by that wretched bed,
    Greater than thou.

Beneath that pauper's roof,
Lo! Death doth keep his state;
Enter, — no crowds attend:
Enter, — no guards defend
    This palace gate.

That pavement damp and cold,
No whispering courtiers tread.
One silent woman stands,
Chafing, with pale, thin hands,
    A dying head.

No busy murmurs sound;
An infant wail alone:
A sob suppressed, — again
That short, deep gasp, — and then
    The parting groan!

O change! O wondrous change!
Burst are the prison bars!

This moment there, — so low
In mortal prayer, — and now
    Beyond the stars!

O change! stupendous change!
Here lies the senseless clod;
The soul from bondage breaks,
The new immortal wakes, —
    Wakes with his God.
C. Bowles.

THE AGED CHRISTIAN.

"Lord, now lettest thou thy servant depart in peace, according to thy word." Luke ii. 29.

'T is enough, — the hour is come
Now within the silent tomb

Let this mortal frame decay,
Mingled with its kindred clay;
Since thy mercies, oft of old
By thy chosen seers foretold,
Faithful now and steadfast prove,
God of truth and God of love!

Since at length my aged eye
Sees the day-spring from on high!
Those whom death had overspread
With his dark and dreary shade,
Lift their eyes, and from afar
Hail the light of Jacob's star;
Waiting till the promised ray
Turn their darkness into day.

Sun of righteousness, to thee,
Lo! the nations bow the knee;
And the realms of distant kings
Own the healing of thy wings.

See the beams, intensely shed,
Shine on Zion's favored head!
Never may they hence remove,
God of truth and God of love!

MERRICK.

"THE TIME OF THE DEAD."

Rev. xi. 18.

GREAT God! what do I see and hear?
  The end of things created!
Behold the Judge of man appear,
  On clouds of glory seated!
The trumpet sounds, the graves restore
The dead which they contained before:
  Prepare, my soul, to meet him.

The dead in Christ shall first arise,
   At the last trumpet's sounding,
Caught up to meet him in the skies,
   With joy their Lord surrounding;
No gloomy fears their soul dismay;
His presence sheds eternal day
   On those prepared to meet him.

But sinners, filled with guilty fears,
   Behold his wrath prevailing;
For they shall rise, and find their tears
   And sighs are unavailing:
The day of grace is past and gone;
Trembling they stand before the throne
   All unprepared to meet him!

Great God! what do I see and hear?
   The end of things created!
Behold the Judge of man appear,
   On clouds of glory seated!

Low at his cross I wait the day,
When heaven and earth shall pass away,
And thus prepare to meet him!

LUTHER.

HEAVENLY REST.

" There remaineth, therefore, a rest for the people of God."—*Heb.* iv. 9.

Sweet is the name of rest!
   How much the word conveys!
It is to be supremely blest
   In the bright world of praise.

It is to rest from sin,
   Which here will still endure;
The holy place to enter in,
   And be for ever pure.

It is to rest from pain,
    From grief, from doubt, from fear:
No sickness. parting, death again,
    Nor any falling tear.

It is to rest with Him,
    Whom now unseen we trust,
With cherubim and seraphim,
    And spirits of the just.

A perfect cloudless rest,
    An endless Sabbath-day;
Blest portion yet to be possessed,
    And never fade away.

HEAVEN.

"And God shall wipe away all tears from their eyes; and there shall be no more death, neither sorrow, nor crying, neither shall there be any more pain; for the former things are passed away." — *Rev.* xxi. 4.

No sickness there, —
No weary wasting of the frame away,
No fearful shrinking from the midnight air,
No dread of summer's bright and fervid ray.

No hidden grief,
No wild and cheerless vision of despair,
No vain petition for a swift relief,
No tearful eyes, no broken hearts, are there.

Care has no home
Within the realm of ceaseless prayer and song;
Its billows break and melt away in foam,
Far from the mansions of the spirit throng.

HYMNS.

The storm's black wing
Is never spread athwart celestial skies;
Its wailings blend not with the voice of spring,
As some too tender floweret fades and dies.

No night distils
Its chilling dews upon the tender frame,
No moon is needed there. The light which fills
That land of glory, from its Maker came.

No parted friends
O'er mournful recollections have to weep;
No bed of death enduring love attends,
To watch the coming of a pulseless sleep.

No blasted flower,
Or withered bud, celestial gardens know;
No scorching blast, or fierce-descending shower,
Scatters destruction like a ruthless foe.

No battle word
Startles the sacred host with fear and dread;
The song of peace creation's morning heard
Is sung wherever angel minstrels tread.

Let us depart,
If home like this await the weary soul.
Look up, thou stricken one! Thy wounded heart
Shall bleed no more at sorrow's stern control.

With faith our guide,
White-robed and innocent, to lead the way,
Why fear to plunge in Jordan's rolling tide,
And find the ocean of eternal day.

THE FAMILY IN HEAVEN AND EARTH.

"Of whom the whole family in heaven and earth is named." — *Eph.* iii. 15.

Come, let us join our friends above,
　That have obtained the prize;
And on the eagle wings of love,
　To joy celestial rise.

Let saints below in concert sing,
　With those to glory gone;
For all the servants of our King
　In heaven and earth are one.

One family, we dwell in him;
　One church above, beneath;
Though now divided by the stream,
　The narrow stream, of death.

One army of the living God,
  To his command we bow;
Part of the host have crossed the flood,
  And part are crossing now.

Each moment, to their endless home,
  Some parting spirits fly;
And we are to the margin come,
  And soon expect to die.

Dear Saviour, be our constant guide,
  Then, when the word is given,
Bid death's cold flood and stream divide,
  And land us safe in heaven.
C. Wesley.

THOUGHTS OF ETERNITY.

"And fulfil all the good pleasure of his goodness, and the work of faith with power." — 1 *Thess.* i. 11.

Thou God of glorious majesty,
To thee, against myself, to thee,
 A worm of earth, I cry;
A half-awakened child of man;
An heir of endless bliss or pain;
 A sinner born to die!

Lo! on a narrow neck of land,
'Twixt two unbounded seas, I stand,
 Secure! insensible!
A point of time, a moment's space,
Removes me to that heavenly place,
 Or shuts me up in hell.

O God, mine inmost soul convert,
And deeply on my thoughtless heart
   Eternal things impress!
Give me to feel their solemn weight,
And save me ere it be too late,
   Wake me to righteousness.

Before me place in dread array
The pomp of that tremendous day,
   When thou with clouds shalt come
To judge the nations at thy bar;
And tell me, Lord, shall I be there
   To meet a joyful doom?

Be this my one great business here,
With holy diligence and fear
   To make my calling sure;
Thine utmost counsel to fulfil,
And suffer all thy righteous will,
   And to the end endure.

Then, Saviour, then my soul **receive,**
Transported from this vale, to live
    And reign with thee above;
Where faith is sweetly lost in sight,
And hope in full, supreme delight,
    And everlasting love.

WESLEY.

www.ingramcontent.com/pod-product-compliance
Lightning Source LLC
Chambersburg PA
CBHW020914230426
43666CB00008B/1456